Esteban's Conclusions
The Seeker's Journal

Dearest Peter,
Thank you so much
for having me,

much love,
erfan

ERFAN DALIRI

Text copyright © Erfan Daliri 2013
Illustrations copyright © Dr Farvardin Daliri OAM

Published by Vivid Publishing
A division of the Fontaine Publishing Group
P.O. Box 948 Fremantle
Western Australia 6959
www.vividpublishing.com.au

ISBN: 978-1-922204-60-8
Cataloguing-in-Publication data is held at the National Library of Australia.

To order further copies of this book or to contact the author, please visit
www.vividpublishing.com.au/estebansconclusions for further information.

Ten thousand moments of hindsight will never amount to a single moment of clarity in the present,

For all my hindsight can now provide is memories of decisions that I now resent,

Regret, repent, reminisce, and then pretend they did not happen,

But they did, and as I sit, with pen in quivering hand, trying to reconcile the discrepancies between my life and my plans,

I find that my tears flow as freely as my words,
And though I wish for my Love to be heard,

Those with the ears that needed to hear these words are no longer here,

And so these pages must now bear the burdens of my soul and carry the weight of my fears.

Forgive me for not holding your hand as tightly as I should have.

I

The clouds have been waiting patiently for an audience with us for many years,

Yet oblivious to the fact I had remained, as I gazed at and bathed in their tears,

Until one night as I sat on the edge of my mind, looking upon the sky with my inner eye,

The clouds, they spoke forth with such force, their wish I could no longer deny,

They said,

O ye moving form of dust! Have you forgotten that we were once as one? Do you not recall the journey we once took from the sun?

Destined to land upon the branch of the tree, you became the apple and I the humble leaf,

The apple it was eaten to become one with your form, and I the leaf, in my longing for you, grew forlorn,

I threw myself from the branch but I was not caught by the graces of the wind, so I fell to the ground,

The moisture was ripped from my body as I screamed out your name, but you heard not my sound,

My form, it became one with the earth, my soul was returned to the atmosphere to rejoin the souls of my fallen peers,

Together we merged to form the clouds, and so it is that for all of these years we have watched you from here,

Lifetimes have passed and still we continue to cry, even as the ocean does heave and sigh,

As all of existence moves from one form to the next, still you fail to pause for but one moment to reflect,

Upon the oneness of our being and all that we have seen,

My dear friend I beg of you, call to mind the memories of all that we have been.

II

We are the flying fish of the eternal ocean of the spiritual world, as waves across these waters we are constantly hurled,

This ocean is both our origin and our destination, from where we receive our sustenance and our greatest inspirations,

These waters they hold us, support and protect us, they feed us and bleed us, never will they reject us,

And we, the flying fish, leap out of the spiritual world to enter physical existence,

For a split second, a passing moment, we leave the realm of weightlessness to enter the realm of resistance,

Confused by our state of contradiction, gasping for the oxygen of unconditional Love, we are blinded by the light,

For we were swimmers in the world of spirit, but we wished to experience the fearful adrenaline rush of flight,

We are separated momentarily as we take this flight alone, we forget of our oneness with the ocean, our eternal home,

And just as swift as the twinkle of a star, we crash back into the ocean's open arms,

Before we can come to understand where we were and what we were to do,
We return to the soul of the universe, the only home we ever knew,
There we are once again reminded of the interconnected nature of our being,
And we will recount to the ocean the stories of all the things we have seen,

During that split second we call a lifetime,

We will look up at the surface from within the sea, and consider the ripples we caused upon our re-entry,

For that is all that remains from this transitory life,
A few ripples that spread out, merge with others, then disappear like a thief in the night,

Not a breath of our words will survive the ocean's tempest, and of significance and meaning our life's work will be bereft,
If not carried out in remembrance of the realm of spirit from which we leapt,

Our fanciful flight only too soon comes to an end, the journey is complete,
But once again from the joy of our reunion, out of the ocean of spirit we leap,

For we are the flying fish of the eternal oceans of the spiritual world,
And as waves across these waters we will be forever hurled.

III

It is your blessed beauty that I seek, it is for your presence that I weep,

Thoughts of a Love such as yours continue to move me towards the day that we meet,

But I ask, how can such an imperfect being bear witness to such a perfect scene?

How can one still riddled with guilt lay eyes upon one of such esteem?

Must I find your beauty within myself before we can be as one? Must the moon recognise her light as a reflection of the sun?

Will your heart also ache if I fall short? Will I be forgiven for the time I have taken and all I've done wrong?

For my hand, it quivers and my heart does ache, as I reflect upon the mistakes I did make,

My ink does run as my tears do flow, how much longer must I remain in this state?

I see glimpses of you every which way I turn, though I know not whether to be patient or to more earnestly yearn,

Must I be still for you to come to me? Or must I like the moth continue to burn?

Last night the breeze was carrying your scent, I stood still, he came up to touch my face,

He told me he was with you not long before, but he would not tell me at which place,

I asked the breeze if he could please leave your blessed scent with me,

He laughed aloud to gather the clouds then said, 'Never! This scent I will forever keep,

To remind you of that which you have lost, I will revisit you from time to time,

So you may revisit the memories of all of the lovers you foolishly declined,'

He held me for a moment and whispered all of their names into my ear,

And then, just as swiftly as he had arrived, the breeze, he disappeared,

I cried out for him to return, but alas he did not,

Instead the moon stepped out from behind the clouds and she spoke forth,

She said,

Cease your tears my sweet child, for these clouds do break each time you cry,

And though your tears fill rivers and streams, this grieving will not take you to meet with your dreams,

First you must build for yourself a raft, so ask of the trees that have fallen in your path,

If of their bodies you may craft, a vessel to carry you away from the ways of your past,

Let the river take you unquestioningly, sing her praises as she carries you to the sea,

So your brothers and sisters may hear your call, that they too may come home to me once more,

Where the mouth of the river meets the wet kiss of the ocean's waves,
Disembark from your vessel and for one final moment reflect upon your days,

And then before the earth turns her back to the sun,
Step into the ocean's waters that the story of your life may come undone,

Drown yourself in her loving embrace, let her wash you of the scars of your heart and those on your face,

Dive into her depths, never look back at the surface, close thine eyes to thyself,
That you may open them to Oneness.

Why is the light at the end afraid to step into the tunnel? Why does the spinning coin so entice us all?

When the breeze blows does it know of its destination, or is it just wandering, wondering from where it has come and to where it will go?

When the river flows, does it remember the time that it was once snow?

Do the clouds gather knowingly in order to watch the spectacle of our lives,

Or do they happen to gather by chance, and in the joy of their reunion do they cry?

What becomes of the soul of the moth once it has completely burnt?

Where does innocence go when it is lost? And what becomes of lessons that were never learnt?

Have you ever wondered how far your breath travels once it has left your lungs?

Or what will become of all of the songs that were written but never sung?

Will those words ever be heard? Will they come to the mind of another?

Is an orphaned child still not a child? Is a childless woman still not a mother?

How far will my words carry their sense of purpose before they fall upon deaf ears?

Should I calculate my age by the number of years I've been alive or how many I've actually lived?

Does concrete remember which of its parts were cement and which were sand once it has set?

Does the sword feel remorse for all the hearts it has caused to have bled?

Do the anvil and the hammer forge the sword lovingly or with hateful rage?

What will become of my pen when it no longer has the company of this page?

For it to rest upon, run along, to explore the far reaches of my mind,

What will become of my unfulfilled dreams once I have run out of time?

Where do my hopes go to once they have been relieved of their post's,

Will they retire comfortably or follow me in the shadows like restless ghosts?

The clouds they spoke to me
They told me, they showed to me
Some things I had never seen
A place I had never been

They said 'You, will never be
Free from the likes of me
For we are inextricably
Intertwined until the end of time

'For now, you walk, I fly
But soon we both will cry
And you, will drink my tears
And they, will quench your fears

'And in their place you'll see
How we, are inextricably
Intertwined until the end of time
For your heart, my dear, is mine'

Then time, she turned to me
She said 'You, will learn from me
Soon, of how to be
Free, from fear and doubt'
And then, the sun did shout

He said 'You, you look up now
And I, will show you how
How you, once flew from me
To land, upon the tree'

The tree, then waved its arms
The leaves, they fell upon
The ground, the ground it shook
The wind, the wind it took

The leaves, away from me
It took them to the sea
The sea, she also waved
Anew, a new path she paved

Of Love, to overcome
Fear, and with the sun
She helped the water to
Evaporate again

The water, it cried out
In joy, as it joined the clouds
The clouds, they spoke to me
They said 'Remember me.'

VII

Who is it that awaits in the depths of the dark, come forth and show your face,

For I sought the secrets of the heart and my pen has directed me to this place,

I turned my back to the light at the end, traced my way back to the beginning,

Void of light though my pen doth scribe, I cannot witness the truth latent within,

For these words I carry back from the soul of the universe are but bullet riddled buckets, no more than fanciful verse,

And though in the depths of the tunnel I fill them with naught but the essence of truth,

Upon my return from that realm these words are empty again, and I am left carrying only a fragrance of what I once knew,

For I cannot carry sunlight in my hands, nor can I catch the tears of the skies with my eyes,

So step forth O darkness, from the depth of your cave, I beg thee, let me watch you dance with the light,

Step forth into the light O darkness of my heart, that you may fill the spaces between our souls,

Fill the spaces between our bodies such that no boundaries will ever again be known,

My words cannot convey how earnestly I yearn to rest in the warmth of your embrace,

But I Love my brothers as I love my mothers and I wish for you to meet them, so they too may find peace,

For only then will I be ready to leave this place.

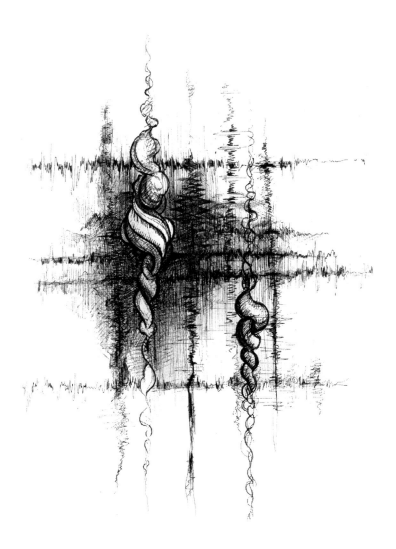

VIII

When a soldier of Love finds need to fight in the name of peace,

Love has already lost,

From that point on, regardless of what the outcome of the battle may be,

War has already won,

When a noble warrior of an ancient tribe decides to bear arms to defend the timeless knowledge of his race,

He forsakes the only portion of that knowledge worth defending in the first place,

The warmongering colonisers, who have wreaked havoc across the face of our mother earth, surely cannot escape blame,

But tell me this, can the arms bearing defendant or the anarchist protestor honestly claim they are not one and the same?

For in any conflict that may arise, hatred has already taken a hold of both sides,

So what is the point of fighting if we have already lost, the only part of us worth keeping?

What honour is worthy of saving, if for its sake even a single life must be taken?

What ideology is worthy of human beings, if conflict and bloodshed is its only means?

I beg of you, choose your means carefully, for in that realm beyond space and time,

Your means is already your end,

And that is why time after time we return to start over from the beginning,

So I ask you my dear friends,

What comfort is worth having, if even a single amongst us cannot partake?

How can any heart be dearer than another, do they not all break?

How can the tears of your child possibly weigh any more than another's?

Do you imagine that perhaps your blood is sweeter than your brother's?

Do the clouds not weep over us all as they watch us from above?

Trying to wash the face of the earth of all of the blood that we have shed in the name of Love,

I am tired, I am weary and I wish to go home, but each time I come to take flight I realise I cannot bear to leave you alone,

I cannot bear to leave you in such a state, divided by imaginary lines into nations,

For while we continue to stand divided not a single one of us will find salvation,

Seek it in your books, your scriptures, your deepest thoughts and your sweetest dreams,

I assure you no peace shall we find, save in the recognition of the singularity of our being,

I Love you my dear friends, though your names I might not know,

I Love you not for who you might be or what you have done for me, but for the fact that we share one soul,

And once you believe that to be so,

Then you will surely come to see that self-defence is no more than a self-contradictory term,

We are harming ourselves when we grieve each other, when will we come to learn,

That justice is not giving someone what you think they deserve, rather what you would give to yourself,

One would imagine, that with all the bloodletting we would have by now shed all of our hate,

Yet we continue to find it and furnish our hearts with it, leaving Love without a place,

To call home,

She wanders the streets at night, homeless and without a place to rest,

She knocks on your door at the break of each new day, still you continue to close the door in her face,

Instead of Love you share your beds with fear, fear of the one you just turned away,

Fear of what you may have had to give up if you had allowed Love to stay,

But Love she wants nothing from you, for Love she has no needs,

Of fear, doubt, shortcomings and uncertainty Love has always been, and will forevermore continue to be free,

For Love has existed before you were born into this realm, and she will continue to exist long after you leave,

You can let Love become of you and you can become Love if you so wish,

Or if you so choose, her existence you can continue to dismiss,

But do not come to me in the dead of night, with your swords washed in blood,

Asking of me to show you the light, when it was you who shunned Love,

For you am I my beloved, when you break my heart you break a piece of yourself,

We are all broken pieces of one broken soul, trapped in separate bodies, this is our hell,

Look yourself in the eye next time she passes by, tell me you don't see your soul in her eyes,

When you stand silently at the bus stop with your soulmates by your side,

Does a part of you not wish to cry?

Do you not see the same pain in their hearts as you feel in yours?

For having stood there without having said a word to your longest lost friend of all,

Yourself?

I tell you now, I only hope that you are ready to believe, I hope that you too wish no more to be the cause of your own grief,

This existence is You, this is Us, this is God, looking at itself,

The brokenhearted single mother of three working two jobs conscientiously,

Is you,

The angry teenager who cuts her arms whenever she gets a moment to be alone,

Is you,

The celibate paedophile who locks himself away in his home, for fear of what he might have done,

Is you,

The actress who numbs herself with drugs, for the pain of the separation of Us,

Is you,

The motherless child begging for scraps of food in the streets of some distant Third World neighbourhood,
Is you,

The ageing billionaire who cries himself to sleep, for the selfish life he has lived,
Is you,

This existence is you looking at yourself,

That is all life has ever been, a vivid self-fulfilling prophecy played out in a dream,
So tell me now, what is it that you see?

Can you see a fast approaching end to this wicked game that we have played?
Can you see the sun rising from behind the mountain of mistakes that we have made?

Do you feel the whisper of the breeze as it comes up to caress your face?
To let you know that you were forgiven even before you realised your mistakes,

Can you see the forest of Love that is waiting patiently within the seed?
Will you plant it in your hearts, will you water it with your deeds?
Will you cleanse your heart and furnish it with Love, will you open wide its doors?
Will you let in every last piece of this broken soul? Or will you leave some pieces of Us to roam in the dark, alone?

For I am growing tired and I wish to go home, but I do not wish to go alone,

So let us, together, run like the river to the sea, let us dance like the breeze with the leaves of the tree,

For knowing we that are one and the same, let us no longer cause ourselves pain,

Let us remember that both the mountaintop and the blade of grass are at once touching the sky,

Let the rivers of blood run dry, let us leave this place of separation behind,

Because the strangest thing about us is that we are still estranged from our self,

For the body of humanity to rest in peace each organ within it must reach the peak of its health,

For God is waiting for us, as the ocean waits for the rain to fall into her open arms,

There is no place else to go but home, so I beg of you my dear friends, let us once again be as one.

IX

If a handful of sand is removed, is the desert no longer the desert?

And if another and yet another are still taken, does that leave the desert as anything less than what it always was?

Furthermore, if that handful of sand was the desert only a moment ago, what is it once removed?

Is it anything less? Or perhaps more?

And what of the single grain of sand? How can it be the desert in one moment and something less the very next?

If it is truth that you seek then find the desert in the single grain of sand,

If it is Love that you seek then search for the ocean within the drop of water,

If it is eternity that you seek then find the vastness of the universe in your own breath, for they are one and the same,

Within each seed does a forest grow, within each drop of your blood lies the script of your form,

What separates the seed from the forest is no more than the passing of time,

Just as the truths of the universe lay latent within these fanciful rhymes,

For these words, they existed long before I placed them in this particular order, yet only with the passing of time could you hear,

Just as God exists everywhere and at all times, but it seems only with moving away can we draw near,

For within each seed awaits a tree and within that tree await a thousand blossoms,

Within those blossoms await tens of thousands more seeds, and in each of those seeds awaits another thousand forests,

If it is the face of God you wish to witness, then let your mind rest in darkness,

If it is the voice of God you wish to hear, then let your ears rest in silence,

If it is the Love of God you wish to feel, then let your heart rest in peace,

And if it is the presence of God you wish to experience, then rest peacefully and of your body be free,

For God is the desert, and I am the single grain of sand, yet which is which is a truth only the true lover can understand,

God is the ocean, and I am the drop of rain, but who is who is a question only the silence can explain,

Then God becomes the silence, and I, the single sound, but who hears who is a knot only the deaf can unbound,

For God is time, and I am a single moment, but to ask which lasts longer will take one to their mind's edge and throw them over,

Look truly my friend, and you will find that the future and the past are sitting side by side,

It is we who squeeze ourselves in-between to pass the present moment with a longing sigh,

And I tell you, the darkness, it goes nowhere when the light begins to shine,

The darkness and the light lovingly agree to fill one another as they both resign to being blind,

Blind to the light that separates thought from form, blind to the dark that separates known from unknown,

For the bird of life flies neither from past to future, nor future to past, she flies for the sake of life and the solace of her heart,

Because from the vastness of the open skies, through which the bird flies, he can clearly see,

How the river is in the very same moment standing at the foot of the mountain and sitting by the sea,

And the river, he bleeds himself selflessly that he may be reunited with the sky,

That he may once again reach the mountaintop as the clouds begin to cry,

And the clouds, O how they weep for all that they have come to witness,

As they watch this ephemeral form searching for the motion of God in the silent stillness.

X

I am what I am

I will not be what I was

Nor will I do what I've done

For secrets will unravel

Lies will come undone

I am what I am

My truths will be told

I paid dearly to purchase

The soul I had once sold

I am what I am

I am not what you think

Nor what you thought

I am free to create

For I no longer believe

What we were once taught

I am what I am

I will become as I choose

The Master of my Universe

I am all, I have naught to lose

I am what I am

I care not who you choose to be

I will speak as I feel

Think with my heart

My Love is true

For whomsoever chooses to see.

XI

Sadness is resting upon the bed of my heart, and though I wish from her to part,

I dare not disturb her from slumber, for I fear she will cause me more grief as she departs,

For we have become accustomed, her and I, not a night have I spent without her by my side,

Together we watch the sun fall from the edge of the earth, that to the stars our lamentations we may confide.

XII

In your tears does God swim, shed them freely and let them wash you of your grief,

But if you find the strength to hold firmly the pen, the brush or the girth of the drum,

Then shed your grief in the chanting of your song,

Let others hear of the song of your blessed heart,
That from where your story meets its end they may start,

Let the falling of the rains of your pain give bloom to sweet scented flowers in the fields of their souls,

That they may be guided away from the darkness you faced and perchance forge a path of their own,

And though grief and sorrow will one day too fill their hearts to the brim,

Worry not my dear child, for in their tears too will God swim.

XIII

Two things come together
Of their union, something new is born

This entity exists for some time
Fulfills a certain purpose, but soon it is gone

For when its time comes to an end
It must again separate into two forms

Each going its own way
To return to its eternal home

Seed meets earth
In time, a tree is formed
With light and water
A leaf is born

The leaves dance in the breeze
Offering shade to those in need

Changing hue with the emotions of the season
Whispering to us the secrets of God's reason

And when autumn comes these leaves will fall
To be wrapped in the earth's embrace once more

What came from the earth will return to the darkness of the soil, but have no fear,
For that part, which was of water, will be stripped from the leaf and returned to the atmosphere,

Just as our bodies and souls become connected in this transitory form,
They serve a purpose and when time comes they separate once more,

The body will return to water and earth, and with light they will once again become fruits,

Upon the limbs of the tree of life their existence will forever continue,

Our souls, just as the moisture that is removed from the fallen leaves,

Will disjoin from our bodies and from this bondage they will again fly free,

I ask you now,

Did the soul of the leaf not already exist, before it was assigned to the body of the leaf?

Will it not exist for evermore?

And furthermore,

Will the clouds judge the leaf in how it spent its time with the tree? Will they disallow it entry to that realm above?

Will they inquire as to what it has done right or insist upon retribution for all it has done wrong?

Will the clouds, for even a moment, question whether that droplet belongs?

Or will that droplet be instantly at one with the sky, the moment it leaves the leaf,

This universe offers us our answers in each and every breath that we ungraciously take, if only we were ready to believe,

Our souls will return to rejoin the soul of the universe, our bodies will return to rejoin the earth,

And so I beg of you my beloved, in the time these two entities are together, do with them something of worth,

But fear not my friend, for if you feel that there is more that you wish to learn,

You may whenever you so wish, return.

31

XIV

It is lonely up here, I can clearly see your souls but I cannot make out your faces,

The air is thin up here, I can hear your cries but I cannot hear your rejoices,

It is cold up here, I am closer to the sun but his light passes through me,

As the breath of the songstress through the hollow reed,

I can hear the voice of God from here, but her Love is so pure it causes my heart to break,

And so this mountain I sit atop told me she will hold out her dress, like that of an ecstatic spinning dervish,

That my words and my tears may flow from my eyes and one day they may meet with yours,

But I wonder, when the river runs to the sea, does he know he is running towards the source?

Do you?

Will you too become the river that bleeds itself dry? Do you not wish for reunion with the open skies?

Will you make of your actions a worthy ink, will you use as a page this thing we call life?

You applaud me when I speak to you from atop this stage, but on the streets you obliviously pass me by,

How dearly I wish to throw myself off of this cliff, but I'm afraid if I do I might fly,

For if I fly I feel I may never again return, my soul is weary of this earthly form, I wish to go home,

I have squeezed my soul into this body 808 times, I've cried, lied, bled and even taken lives,

On this quest to purify heart and my soul, that I may become light enough to transcend peacefully into the next world,

But as I stand here watching you from afar, I dare not leave you alone,

For I fear if I go home without you, I will once again have to return,

For without your wandering sages and your lonely poets, to whom would you turn when you need solace?

Without your estranged philosophers watching you from afar, who would you ask your questions of when you wish to know who you truly are?

Without your silent contemplative types, to whom would you turn when you seek advice?

If the candle were to not sacrifice itself in becoming light, who would be your guide during the soul's darkest of nights?

Without penniless artists thickening their paints with their own blood, who would paint you your maps, who would offer to you directions to Love?

It is bright up here my friends, so bright in fact that one goes blind, blind to the differences you continue to find,

Blind to the lines you choose to draw between one another,

So I urge you leave the drawing and the painting, the writing and the singing to the artists amongst us,

For the artist seeks only to draw images that you may witness beauty with the eye of your mind,

While you draw your swords from their sheaths to draw the blood of these brothers of mine,

But if you were to look at this world from where I stand, you would see only One, one entity in conflict with itself,

You would see a hand cutting itself off at the arm and a head that decides to amass more arms,

For I have watched the mouthpiece of civilisation chew its own fingers off,

I have seen workers feeding the bloated stomach of the world, left hungry, homeless, sleeping in the cold,

I have seen legs, skinny and frail, soon to collapse under the weight of your gluttonous ways,

I can hear God begging you to cease your slaughter of each other, for the way another chooses to pray,

I have seen eyes rolled back into the skull, blind to the light of the sun,

I have seen a thirsty mouth cutting its own throat that it may drink its own blood,

Silently I watched your coronation of lust, for I was amongst the banished prisoners when you exiled Love,

I have seen ribs shattered and broken, piercing the heart they were to protect,

I have seen far too many lives lost to ignorant neglect,

I watched as the dove clipped its own wings for the sorrow of having forgotten how to sing,

And now I can hear the nightingale of life weeping upon the bow of the tree of life, I wish no more to be witness to such things,

It is lonely up here and though I wish to leave, my Love for you keeps me here until the day our knowledge meets our belief,

And so I continue to return time and again, that the seeker may find the true friend,

That the lover and the beloved may find one another,

O how I yearn to witness that moment they realise they have always been One, and the same.

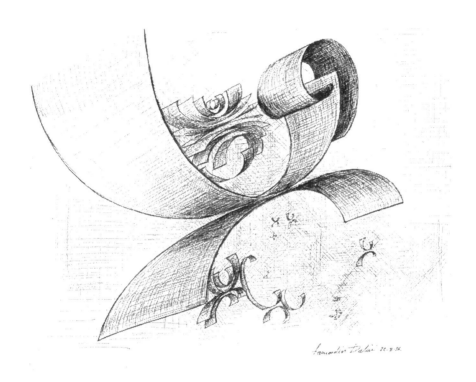

Samuel Dalí 22.9.36.

XV

The Truth is,

The Truth simply is,

The simple truth is, that the Truth has always been, everywhere and ever-present at all times,

For the Tuth is the line upon which is scribed the story of our lives,

The Truth cannot hide nor can it be hidden, though it can be denied by the eyes of those who wish to not yet see it,

You cannot possible exclaim 'show me the Truth!' and for her to remain unseen,

For the Truth, she waits patiently to be witnessed by whomsoever chooses to see,

And confusion is no more than a state of mind that we enter willingly on our quest for greater clarity,

If you settle, as does the earth in a pool of still water, you will find the answers that you have, for so long, searched for,

And our searching is not so much an arduous task, as it is the simple recognition and acceptance of our flawed past,

So pull your awareness from past and future back to this present moment,

Take responsibility for your current situation and the story of your life and decide to own it,

Only then can the Truth be witnessed and experienced in her fullest glory,

From that point onwards you will become the sole scriptor of your own story,

For the Truth does not answer to longing sighs or incessant whines,

If you wish to be free from the torment of your own lies, then show courage and fortitude in the face of your greatest fears,

For only then will the Truth oblige,

You see the Truth is not a guarded secret, nobody can preach it, there exists none who can teach it,

The Truth does not retreat, nor does it wait behind fortified castle walls,
The Truth is a faithful hawk, wishing to rest upon your shoulder at the sound of your call,

It may have been quite some time since you have seen her, heard of her, or even mentioned her name,
But she is at all times present, encompassing both night and day, for the Truth, she is the life and the way,

If you were to but clear your hearts of fear and hate, and look with pure eyes at anything within this universe,
You will see the Truth smiling at you, pleased that you finally decided to witness her,

Sitting naked in the greatness of her glory at the shores of true knowledge, greeting the arrivals as they throw themselves in,
To the depths of the breast of the ocean of faith, to find the priceless gems latent within.

How many times must I go around the block before I can say 'I've been around the block a few times'?

How many lines must I scribe that I may compensate for all of my lies?

How many lives must I live before I learn how to live? How many chances must I be given before I learn how to unconditionally give?

How many lovers must I lose before I learn how to Love? How many hearts must I break before we can get back to Us?

How many more tears must I shed before I can say that I've bled?

O for the nights I have lain awake and cried, how many more must I endure before I can say 'At least I tried'?

How many more languages must I understand before I learn how to speak?

How many more kicks to the gut must we take before we learn to be meek?

How humble must the seeker become before he is allowed to see?

How many Gods must I worship before God finally acknowledges me?

How many more pages must be filled before no more blood needs be spilled?

How many more books must line these shelves before we realise the bookcase was already full?

How many more lovers will I forsake before my heart can take no more?

How many more locks must I pick before I can finally open the door?

How many sunsets must I watch alone before I can watch the sun rise?

How many times must I apologise that I may be forgiven for my past lives?

How many betrayers must I forgive before I myself am forgiven?

How much longer will we endure this slow and painful death before we start living?

How many times must I give a hand before someone will take mine?

How many more clocks must I destroy before I learn how to turn back time?

How many shooting stars must I watch before I learn how to make a wish?

How many more wishes must I grant in order to save the world of its anguish?

How many more years must I continue to travel before I can rest for the night?

For how long must I retreat into my cave that I may see the light?

How much longer must I remain in this silent darkness for my eyes to adjust?

How many more times will I mistake the harbinger of Love for the temptress of lust?

How many childhood memories must I erase before I can have children of my own?

How many more houses must I break into before I can find a place to call home?

How many audiences must applaud my words before I believe what I say?

How many more temples must I desecrate before I remember how to pray?

How many lives must be lost for us to acknowledge that we've lost the plot?

How many stitches will we need once we cut out the parts of ourselves that have begun to rot?

What does a man do when he is afraid of his dreams?

Not because of the heart-wrenching screams that had plagued him once before,

But because he was now sure,

That the power of his mind and the potency of his soul had created his universe, from big bang to black hole,

What if his imaginings by night were unfolding day by day, and he no longer had to pray but simply say,

'Be' and it would come to be,

Would you believe him or would you refuse to see?

What if he was afraid to dream not because of that which he had seen,

But because he felt perhaps it was he who had dreamt these things into being?

What if it was as a result of his own thought that the children had not been taught of the singularity of their existence?

What if it was his mind that had created war and conflict, revolution and resistance?

What if it was his own blindness that had blinded the people, and led them to kill in the name of the church steeple?

What if he was now beyond a shadow of a doubt certain, that it was he who had withheld himself from the truth that waited behind the curtain?

What if his mind was what controlled his health, and his mental projections had separated the self from The Self?

I tell you now I too was once afraid to dream, not because of what I might see,

But because I realised it was I who created my reality,

How can one bear the responsibility of such a task? Why bestow one with a power for which they did not ask?

Perhaps I asked for it in a lifetime past, if only I could remember what happened the time before last,

What I do remember is that creation was an act of creativity, and this God they speak of is not the external father, but rather the collective sum of you and me,

I also remember that my reality is virtually brought to be by what I choose to dream,

The question remains, what then are we supposed to dream? How can we imagine that which has remained unseen?

I was afraid to dream because I knew I'd dreamt before, I was afraid to sleep because I did not know to where I would go,

Do I go home each time I close my eyes, or is there a gatekeeper who judges and denies,

Entry to those who dreamt not of the truth from which we came?

They say we go to heaven or hell, but my heart says we're all the same,

Yet each time I speak of my idea of unconditional Love, they say 'Son, you've gone insane,'

The preacher says that there is a good and bad, my psychiatrist insists that there is right and wrong,

And everyone else says 'You have to believe in my God if you want to belong,'

These judgments being made were confining the breathing of my heart,

The walls of that room were moving closer together, as the rest of my universe was moving further apart,

So as I sat strapped in that white walled room, wanting to cry out but not knowing to whom,

I was kept company by a poet called Rumi, he knew me like no one else ever knew me,

He wrote to me four hundred years ago, this for you I will elaborate very slow,

Outside of your ideas of good and bad, just beyond the mountain range of right and wrong, lies a beautiful valley where you will fulfill your heartsong,

Where the flowers of Love sway in the breeze of an unjudging wind,

Where you will find that the Glory of God is emanating from everything,

That is where you will find me, that is where for you I have waited,

This place you call hell, you're already in it, and it is by you that it was created,

So I say to you now, dream the unseen and sing the unheard, be the bow and arrow or be the bird,

For it matters not what you choose to be, rather it only matters that we realise the essence of true unity,

So touch the untouchables, Love the unlovables, mention the unmentionable and stop the unstoppable, move the immovable and imagine the unimaginable,

Do as you wish and wish as you please, but please continue to dream, for I dream that one day, we dream the same dream,

You see,

Your pain is my sin, and my sin is your growth,
Your growth gives me wings, my wings your re-birth,
Your re-birth is my death, my death to this earth,

At my ascension from which my soul will fly high,
And we will finally realise that my soul is your soul and your soul is mine.

XVIII

I am both honoured and humbled for having been given a voice with which to speak,

But if my complete honesty is what you wish to witness, then I must also admit,

That in my heart of hearts I am saddened, not for the opportunity granted, for this life is a blessed gift,

But for the fact that there is nothing left for me to say, nothing left for which one can pray,

Nothing that is, that has not already been said, nothing that we have not already been told,

Nothing we have not already seen, heard or observed, nothing we have not already ignored,

Any utterance to which I may lay claim, would merely be a transliteration of something we have already known,

The repetition of something we have already been told, many times, and long ago,

Time and time again, my friends, we make the same mistakes, my friends,

And each time we get close to the end, we lose our way and end up at the beginning again,

Because of the language in which others choose to pray, we burn our brother's ancient libraries,

We rape our mother earth and widow our sisters, I don't know why this is,

For we have been through this before many times my friends,
Do you recall Lemuria and Atlantis?

XIX

If I should have a son I would call him Esteban, because it means 'The Crowned One,'
And if he should ask me of the ways of the soul I would say 'ask your mum, for she is the crowned one,'

You see we both have hearts but her heart is a little bigger, she will teach you how to Love without condition and help you see things a little clearer,

For she is the one who gave birth to you, just as the earth gave birth to us all,
But men, they cut their mother up into nations and carve scars into her face with their resource-based wars,

Men send their sons to fight for the honour of their country, and as long as they die gloriously,
They don't care if they return at all,

Men think their mother tongue is the only one, they think their motherland can be lost and won,
So if I were to have a son,

I would teach him a woman's heart is not a holy relic to be seized like the spoils of a victor,
Though it can seize with grief if ever you neglect her,

A woman's heart, my child, is a temple you must approach with reverent respect,
It needs no banner to be planted in its soil to claim your name or intent,

A woman's heart is the home to which you belong, but you must first become worthy if you wish to enter,
The walls of that heart will protect you eternally when you learn to respect her,

A woman's heart can be as fragile as a snowflake and yet as resilient as a fortress wall,

As sweet as the breath of a newborn child, and just like the sign on the china store door,

'If you break it, you will pay for it,'

In this lifetime or the next, or the one after that, you'll keep coming back until you learn to Love like a woman can,

If I were to have a son I might wish for a daughter, and if I were to have a daughter I might wish for a son,

But a mother loves her children no matter how they come, or who they choose to do so with,

If I were to have a son I would place him on my shoulders so he could look up to his mum,

And I would be there for him like the foundation stone of a home,

But I would ask that from that foundation he builds a castle of his own,

I would shade and protect him from the troubles that may be, but not like an elm, more like a pine tree,

Narrow and straight I will stand, you are protected when you are near but soon you must release your hold of my hand,

That you may venture bravely into the depths of the woods of your own free accord,

Plant seeds of Love along the way as Hansel did, that when you get lost you may find your way back to the source,

I will not plant my own seeds of fear and doubt in his heart, for that garden is his to nurture and look after,

And for as long as that heart beats to the rhythm of life and those blessed lungs breathe deep of limitless Love,

How he chooses to furnish his heart is up to him,

I would advise him and guide him but not like a tyrant, more like the wind,

I would whisper to him the things I have learnt, and just as swiftly as the breeze I would leave him alone,

To the privacy of his mind, that he may himself decide if he wishes to fly, cry, burn or grow,

I would ask him to not turn his back to the sun and cast shadows before him,

But no matter what he chooses to do on this earth I will continue to adore him,

I would shower him with Love such that his heart had space to carry nothing else,

I would tell him that this world is not our oyster, we are just borrowing it, so do with it something of worth,

Do not grieve when you feel alone, for you are a particle of God and alone you can never be,

So let your Love act as gravity and pull all the other particles back together again, for God is spelt W, E,

Let your Love flow to others like the river to the sea, infinite, eternal and unconditionally,

If I were to have a son I would ask him to Love others like they were his mothers,

His sisters and his brothers, and to never ask the name of another before you have said 'I Love You',

But to remember that when others say it, it doesn't always mean it's true,

And though your heart may break along the way, it will heal itself no matter to whom you may pray,

As long as you pray every now and then, but not when you're grieving only pray when,

You are grateful and gracious for the hardships you were given,

Be wary but do not grow weary, for we are all on different parts of our journey,

And though some people may say things that you may not necessarily believe,

You should let them know that you Love them regardless before you leave,

Do not ever consider anything as inherently right or wrong, instead ask yourself if it is false or true,

And by that I mean, is that thought, action or emotional response a true reflection of you,

And if it is not, then don't do it again,

Never criticise what others may do, for that is their decision and its judgment is not for you,

You have your own path and no one else can take it, others have theirs and you cannot change it,

Always remember to stay true to yourself, share with others when you meet with wealth,

And when you have nothing, be content,

I would ask of him to keep his heart clean that he may rest peacefully,

And to keep his home clean that he may never step on an ant accidentally,

Do not spray poisons into the air that we share to rid it of mosquitos or flies,

For they too have a purpose, no greater or lesser than yours or mine,

Instead find your purpose and fill it to your hearts content, for that is the only way to true fulfillment,

Never overeat for that is ungracious and unfair, always be a little hungry just to show that you care,

For those who have less than you to eat, for one day you may find yourself at their feet,

And when you do, kiss those blessed feet and ask of them for nothing in return,

Because if it is of true Love that you wish to learn then it may be asked of you to burn,

For the moth was not actually in Love with the flame, it was in truth in Love with the bird,

It danced the maddening dance of Love with the fire that the smoke of its wings could rise to the next world,

If I were to have a son I would help him to sharpen his blade that he may cut himself free,

But I would teach him to never point that blade at another for we are only the masters of our own destiny,

But if one should arise who wishes to cause you harm or desires to take your life, then hand it over freely and be sure to do it with a smile,

For though your soul is eternal and it can never die, your body is yours for only a while,

If I were to have a son I would wish for him to have his mother's eyes,

And I would wish that his forefathers may watch over him from the skies,

And though I do not yet know who his mother might be,

I will continue to burn and purify myself, that his mother may recognise me.

XX

I've spent a lifetime searching for someone, but I don't know what she looks like,

I keep searching anyway, hoping I might recognise her from a past life,

I might not know what she looks like, but I do know how she feels in my arms,

I don't know her name, but I do know the sound of her voice,

For we have spoken many times, my lover and I, sometimes she whispers and other times she screams,

She says 'Hurry my dear, wake up! This existence is but a fleeting dream,

When will you cease your wandering and your wondering, when will you wing your way home?

We have children my dear, they are waiting patiently to be born,'

I know she speaks the truth, for I too have spoken with my children,

They come to me in dreams and say, 'Dear father when will you release hold of your pen?'

I reply 'Soon my dear child, soon I shall oblige, for soon shall come a time when fear will have no place to hide,

I know you too have a purpose, I know that your soul is restless to return to this earthly form,

Your mother has told me that you are waiting for a body into which you may be born,

'But this world is not yet ready for one such as you my child, I am preparing the way as swiftly as I can,

This world is still too cruel, it is still full of fear, this world is still too dark for one such as you my dear,

'Not that I would ever wish for you to avoid the darkness my dear child, nay,

Rather I worry that your light be so bright you will only too soon set this world ablaze,'

Then I turn in my sleep, in my next dream I again speak with their mother,

I ask,

'What is your name my Love? Will you tell me one day soon? Will you know me when we meet, or is it I who must recognise you?

Step forth from my dreams my Love, I beg you step forth, step into the light of my days,

For I have spent 808 lifetimes and twenty-nine years trying to find my way out of this maze,'

Time and again my dreamtime comes to an end, and when sleep leaves confusion sets in,

Such that I cannot be sure if I am moving much too fast or not fast enough,

I cannot be sure if I am finding myself, or only getting myself further lost,

I cannot be sure if I am running, swimming or flying sometimes,

Because I've crossed too many lines and diluted the Truth with my own lies,

I've caused far too many mothers to cry, and still I'm not sure exactly why,

I have had to come back to this place so many times,

Perhaps I chose to return so I could once again gaze upon my true lover's face,

If only I knew what she looked like, maybe it was my ex-wife, maybe in the next life,

Maybe I'll keep coming back until the day I find the courage to take my own life,

I don't know, I can't be sure, maybe when I finally pick the lock and open the door,

I will realise that I was already standing on the inside, maybe then I will understand why I lied,

Why did I have to make her cry? I know she truly loved me but her light was too bright, so within the darkness I decided to hide,

And then again I hear that familiar voice speaking to my unborn child,

She says 'Worry not my dear, your father will soon be home, for light cannot hide within the darkness for too long,

So run along my child, run along, your father is almost ready and soon your time will come.'

XXI

I remember falling in Love with the girl who lived in the little
brown house, on the corner of my grandparents' green street,
  Flanked by white rose bushes, the red brick fence was a fortress
wall around a castle surrounded by a moat,

Inside sat a Queen, I was only sixteen, she was probably a
couple of years younger than me,

She had cherry lips and orange freckles scattered like marbles
across the bridge of her olive skinned nose,
  Blue eyes looked out from above pink cheeks, and her blonde
hair waved about in the air as if it were screaming into the wind,

I might have only been a kid but I knew I was in Love, I knew
that my Love was true,
  I don't remember your name my dear, but sometimes I still
think of you,

I knew I was in Love because at one time I would look forward
to visiting my grandparents for reasons other than her,

Like the way my grandfather cooked eggs, it wasn't a secret
recipe but I could never get them to taste the same,

I would look forward to the smell of my uncle's shirts, he
always carried with him the scent of cologne and the musk of cigarettes,
  No matter how wild the party was my uncle would never miss
his father's breakfast,

His car smelt of denim jackets left in the sun, hair product and
chewing gum,
  My grandfather would sit awake at night worrying until he
would hear my uncle's car arrive,

Then he would quietly make his way to his bedroom so my uncle would not realise that he'd been up all night,

And my grandmother, she smelt like the colour white,

White was the colour of the dress that the girl who lived in the little brown house on the corner of my grandparents' green street was wearing, the day my yellow tennis ball landed in her yard,

She was sitting on the front steps, chin resting delicately on her hands with her elbows placed on her knees,

She was pretending to watch the butterflies dance with the breeze,

But I knew she was just waiting for me,

So I hit a cover drive a little too hard, and my tennis ball landed in her front yard,

From that day on it wasn't the smell of my uncle's car, grandpa's breakfast or grandma's hugs that I looked forward to,

But the way that girl's smile changed the colours of my life, sometimes I still miss my ex-wife,

But those memories are becoming grey,

Grey was the colour of my grandfather's hair before it turned white,

White is what my grandmother smelt like.

XXII

Last night an old friend by the of name of Amy came to me in a dream, she said,

'I will show you the secrets of the universe, but to see them you must first step out of your head,'

So I did,

She spoke softly but swiftly, for she knew my consciousness would soon return to my bed,

She opened for me the book of Truth, but alas upon my return I forgot what I'd read,

The secrets lay somewhere between the wavelength and the amplitude of heart and mind,

Along the intricately woven length of string that binds, the ocean to the waves and the clouds to the rain,

Hidden somewhere in the Love hate relationship of joy and pain,

You see joy, she loves pain, for in him she sees the man he could be,

And pain loves joy, for she gives him a reason to be,

But joy hates the way pain treats those around him in times of grief and loss,

And pain hates that after all these years, joy still does not understand, he is just doing his job.

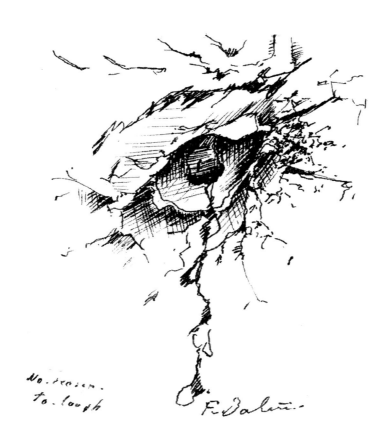

No.frozen.
to.cough

F.Dale

XXIII

There is a place, a place we are all looking for, whether we
know it, feel it, accept it or not, there is a place,
And we are all looking for it,

A place where our lungs breathe deep of the pure clean air,
Where the winds don't blow to destroy homes, but just strong
enough to dance with your lover's hair,

A place where storms no longer unleash torrents of tears,
flooding our streets and minds with fears,
Drowning our hopes and dreams, but fall gently and softly, just
to refill the rivers and streams,

In this place, the clouds, they gather to watch over us as we go
about our days, lingering sometimes into the dusk,
Just to make the sunset that little bit more beautiful to watch,

In this place giants walk with their heads held high, shoulders
back, backs straight, giants walk like you and I,

These giants, they walk with confident intent and deep loving
care,
While gazing towards distant skies, their footsteps are cautious
and aware,
Of where they land, for they wish to cause no harm to any
creature that may tread that same path,

In this place mothers no longer weep for missing husbands,
estranged daughters or dead sons,
They only cry out from the joy of their hearts every now and
then,
Fathers and sons kick footballs and pass knowledge, back and
forth, from future to past,

Mothers and daughters are recognised for the glorious beings that they are,

And siblings no longer fuss and fight, for all they were ever taught was how to laugh,

In this place the moon smiles as she watches us dance into the night,

And in the day the sun warms our hearts and our minds with his light,

In this place we will no longer have to shoot down stars to fulfill our hearts desires,

For our dreams, they would have already arrived, and all of our wishes will be right there next to us,

In this place there will be no longing only be-ing,

We will no longer be wanting or needing, coming, going, trying, waiting or hoping,

We will finally be present in the moment, no matter where we may be,

In this place the single piano note will be left to linger, so the strings of the guitar can dance with our fingers,

And the sounds will travel through the crystal clear paths of our minds,

For music will be the language of discussing the sublime,

In this place Love will exist unbounded by the fear of loss or measured by time,

Love will no longer exist as a yearning in your heart or mine,

Love will be the air that we breathe, the smile we give away for free, the hand that we hold, whoever's it may be,

Love will be the cloth that we wear and the food that we eat, the uninterrupted gaze across the street, though the other may not even see,

In this place grandmothers will no longer sit in the dark corners of their home,

Because in this place nobody eats, sleeps, lives or dies alone,

For in this place we would have finally recognised who we truly are, and our universe will no longer be moving apart,

We will see each other as parts of the One True Self, and no part will be known to have any greater or lesser worth,

In this place we will no longer use the words 'you' or 'I', unless there is a Love in-between,

Like 'I Love you' or 'I am in Love with you' or 'I am Love and so are you,'

In this place the waves are calm and the oceans blue, and the giants that sail these waters are peaceful too,

For they don't travel to conquer new lands or spread their point of view,

These giants sail the waters just because they can,

And the giants that inhabit this space, they don't walk from place to place,

No, they dance when they want to move, just so they can embrace each moment of beauty with open arms, as it comes to pass,

In this place children will be known as Gods, and grown men will play like children, blind to age, colour or race,

And the narrative of God will be a fairytale we frighten men with when they misbehave,

Because in this place women will be our leaders and they will be our guides,

To Love like a woman will be our journey and our destination, our goal, our refuge and our only desire,

When we arrive at this place we would have long left our egos behind, and no one will ever have any reason to lie,

For judgment and misunderstanding will have no standing in such a place,

None will be left begging for food or shunned in disgrace,

Our fears, doubts and shortcomings will no longer be, for we will finally see,

That the infinite can never be anything but infinite, perfectly perfect is what we have always been,

In this place no creature is great or small, just particles vibrating at different frequencies, connected at once to the destination and the source,

I promise you this place does exist, because finding it was the purpose of our existence,

We separated from each other and left home just to test our intuition,

You see we are actually one entity, it just seems as though we are apart,

We created this universe just to test the strength of our hearts,

Don't you remember that time we were as one?

This was meant to be a game, but we've been playing without rules for far too long,

I see looks of worry on some faces, for fear of not knowing where this place is,

But fear it exists here not there, so clear your hearts of all of your fears,

And fill those spaces with Love, that the path ahead may become a little clearer,

I know you too are all looking for this place, it's the reason we all feel so displaced,

The preoccupied father scouring the business section of the paper, while his son waits with his kite in hand,

The mother who loses her cool with her child when her keys cannot be found,

The workers on the buses and trains, the ones stuck in their cars each day,

Frantically going to and from, back and forth, keeping themselves busy, though they may or may not know,

Are all looking for this place,

The racially prejudiced man who kills out of hate, the morbidly obese with too much on his plate,

The hoarders and the nightclub scorers, the ones with ADHD and OCD, the schoolyard bullies that picked on me,

The irritated bus driver, the cheater, the backstabber and the liar, are all looking for this place,

The university professor professing he has found the particle of God, the frantic schizophrenic who seems to have lost the plot,

The alchemist looking for the philosopher's stone, the philosopher still searching for the unknown,

The religious zealot claiming to own the truth, the fundamentalist sacrificing the lives of the youth,

The atheist trying to hide her searching eyes, while the politicians lead our societies to their demise,

By pulling sheets over our heads, expecting us to play dead,

But sometimes these sheets, they end up with holes in them, and those eyes they see only red,

They draw lines between day and night, wrong and right, not realising that the directions to this place were never written in black and white,

But hidden somewhere in the grey, deep within the way the world sways,

Not at the peak or the trough, but finely inscribed along the whole length of the wave,

And those searching for this place the most frantically aren't the ones who Eat, Love, Pray,

They're the ones who drink, snort, suck, pop, lock and sleep all day,

The ones occupied with the most fashionable way to undress themselves or cut their wrists, or their hair,

They are the ones, who are trying the hardest to hide the fact that they still care,

They play their music loud to drown out the screams in their heads,

Do laps up and down the streets just in case they missed something on their last attempt,

They get wasted blind trying to find the light, pop pills, race lines to be the first to find,

This place we are all looking for,

They line up in the cold to get into the dark buildings with the flashing lights, hoping that tonight might just be the night they get it right,

Day in, day out, they're out and about, prowling the streets with shoulders back,

But their heads aren't held so high, they're tilted at an angle of twenty-eight degrees,

Looking for the next victim to bear the brunt of their grief, for not having found this place we all need,

These youths are looking for validation, trying to make sense of their alienation,

From a society that long stopped giving a stuff, just give them cheap alcohol and drugs,

Flashing lights, camera, phones, no action, take their rights, and some more, quell the reaction,

By giving them songs with no more than two lines so they can chant out in the dark like the war cry of a search party,

These animals, they dance from restlessness, not from the joy of their hearts,

And they drink so they won't have to cry, because they know their day jobs are a lie,

They only work during the week, so when the week comes to an end,

They can fund their search for this place we all belong,

A place where we can be whole, content and complete, where we can live peacefully and full of peace,

Where we will finally recognise each other as parts of the One True Self,

Where we can reach the peak of our physical, mental and spiritual health,

And finally lose the ability to differentiate between one another,

Once we find our way to this place we will no longer have to search for anything, for we would have arrived at our truth,

And no one will need to convince another, we will just smile and nod, knowing we both already knew,

And if you were to tell me that you are no longer searching for this place, for you have already found it,

I would look deep in your eyes, take both your hands in mine, and say this,

Lead me… and I will follow, if only for a while,

The least I owe you, is a chance to show me, your way home, because I'm still searching for now.

XXIV

I stood in the midday sun
Still I felt like a shadow
I kissed the loaded gun
But my courage was shallow

I walked amongst flames
Still I felt cold
Injected myself with pain
But I fear I have sold my soul

Could it be that I stand
Too close to my reflection
For me to understand
The truth of my perfection

With face against mirror
I see nothing but black
In order to see clearer
I decide to step back

Then I become too far removed
From the rest of my universe
For me to be soothed
By the truth of my own verse

And so as I stand back, watching from afar
Wishing to know God, and who you all are
Wanting to distinguish sun of reality
From a myriad false stars

I scream at the night sky
An explosion expressed as a sigh
I know I exist
Though I know not why

What I do know is that within the seed sits the forest
And the world's pains in my chest
I know within the drop awaits ocean
And that we are ephemeral at best

So I decide to enter the tunnel, eyes closed, arms out
With the full force of my lungs, I did shout
Who are you that awaits in the grip of this dark?
Why was this lover denied the desire of his heart?

Why must I lose all that I've ever owned
In order to approach Thy blessed home?
Why must I give up my life and my name?
Why must this journey be taken alone?

These things I wish for you to explain
Answer me beast before you are slain
For what reason do I exist?
For what purpose must I burn?

Suddenly a voice did reply,
Because you wished to lose your knowledge that you could once again learn

Of the true nature of the One True Self
And of the nature of true wealth
You chose to forsake all that was false
That you might gain that of true worth

And though weighty burdens you may bear
You must continue on without a care
Until you arrive at the truth
That patiently awaits you, both here and there

So strengthen your faith with proof
Spend wisely the days of your youth
Learn to over look all that is false
That you may look over that which is truth

But who are these beings that surround me?
Are they of you, or perhaps of my dreams?
For I see them though they see me not
Nor do they hear the sound of my screams

Freely they move and speak and dance
But their merriment I fail to understand
Are they nearer to you?
Or so far from you that alone I must stand?

Is it they who are false
Or me who is lost?
Are they the mirage
Or am I the ghost?

They are both and so too are you
You are both fallacy and true
Both mirror and mirage
But alas, those who can recognise this are still too few

For within this world that you exist
You dream into being whatsoever you wish
Though what you chooose to create
I can in nowise insist

Dream of Love and Love you shall see
Dream yourself into a version of Me
But if hell is what you wish to create
Then close thine eyes and dream with hate

What if reality is what I wish to see?
What if I just wish to be free
Of this dream that I may see
Something that is more real than me?

My dear friend there is nothing more real than you
For you am I and I am you
We are one and the same
Together we are the One, the many and the few

For there can only exist but one, there can be no more
The One became the many for We wished to explore
The true nature of the One True Self
But only few remember this truth of all

So find the few others and together unite
That as one your light may shine bright
And the many still seeking peace
May find their way home in this dark night

But why must I bear such a responsibility?
Why can the mountain not be with the sea?
Why must I be the light?
When all that I wish for is to be free?

Because you, my beloved, have already been
All that can be in this vivid dream
You chose to return to those you left
That you could recount to them all that you've seen

For you have been rain, river and sea
And you returned at your own decree
For you wished to be of the ones
Who guided the lovers back to Me

If you were to smile
Then I could smile too
But if you do not smile my dear child
This mirror cannot smile back at you

For this universe is but a mirror
You will see as you draw nearer
That this world exists only
For God to see itself clearer

For God is all that there is, at the end and the start
But wanting to know of the depth of Our heart
The One True Self was separated
And this universe created by being pulled apart

At that point both voices fell silent
And the two of them merged
But my pen it continued to move
As a voice from deep within me emerged

It said,

This separation has been prolonged
And the soul of this seeker now longs
To be reunited with the One True Self
And so he chants out his heartsong

As he wanders through a myriad dreams
Crossing the mountains and the streams
Calling his brothers and mothers home
He cries out, but alas, none hear his screams

For these people have lost their eyes and their ears
Their hearts they have filled with countless fears
They wander without aim through these fields
But the call of this shepherd they fail to hear

O how he weeps for the plight of his soul
For without his brothers he cannot be whole
And then his cries turn to wails as he reflects
Upon the Shepherds who once led him as a foal

How much greater must be Their pain
For seeing Their holy teachings were in vain
They came to bring us peace
But Their words were treated with disdain

In the name of these words each other they slay
These contemptuous fools then sit down to pray
Thinking they belong to the one true faith
While the Shepherds sit together, weeping in grief-stricken dismay.

XXV

I gazed upon the mirror and I found God,

Not in the image reflected, but in the way those atoms hold onto each other to form the mirror itself,
In the way the electron orbits the nucleus, in adoration of the One True Self,

I daydreamt and sleepwalked to the edges of my mind,
I stared into the abyss and called out your name, and the echo called out mine,

You see, we are one and the same, a single entity separated into many,
One form with different names, I am a figment of your imagination, and you a creation of my dreams,

We created this universe ourselves just to test the strength of our Love,
That I could find you and you could find me, as we had promised each other lifetimes ago.

XXVI

My heart, O how it trembled, as I held my nervous pen in my quivering hand,

'Where shall we go today,' I asked 'my dear friends?'

My heart, she spoke forth bravely and said 'To Love let us proceed,'

But my hand it cried out saying 'No! No! It is peace that we most urgently need,'

And my pen, in its grief, it began to bleed,

It said,

Be still O trembling heart, clear your self of desire that Love may make herself known,

And you, my dear hand, hold me tight through the night, for I too wish for peace, you are not alone,

But for as long as life affords you a page, scribe your story my dear friend,

That when your soul returns home, your influence upon this earth may continue without end,

For these pages that carry our words in humble service are numbered, they will not always be here to serve us,

Just as the moth to the flame, these pages too will one day be asked to burn,

That they may become the light, by which others may scribe and come to learn,

Of the true nature of the One True Self, for though your words be sweet, they hold no inherent wealth,

They are merely directions, by which you may find your own way home,

For the journey to oneness is one that must be taken alone,

My heart, O how it wailed, as it heard those words, my tears
formed a stream that gathered the thirsty birds,

    They drank deep and full of the lamentations of my heart, and
in the sweet salt of that flow they heard,

    'Fly straight as the arrow O bird of mine,
Let not your ardour be lost in time,

    For though the wave may peak and trough,
Only in stillness will my secrets untwine,

    'For desire is but a veil the lonely heart shrouds itself in,
A veil that must burn for the journey of the soul to begin,

    For whilst under the cover of lust,
The heart shall not witness the truth of Love that lies within,

    'And though this unveiling may be the cause of much pain,
It must needs be done if your fears are to be slain,

    For these waves of Love and fear that we traverse,
Have driven many a seasoned sailor insane.'

XXVII

How many divergent paths must we take?

For how much longer must we travel down these seemingly differing paths, before we realise that the destination can only ever be one and the same?

And furthermore that the destination is the origin, the beginning is an end, and the alpha has always been the omega?

How many lives must we live and how many more must we take before we finally comprehend the simple truth of the statement 'We are One'?

How many more souls will we falsely claim to have been damned to hell or believe to have acquired salvation in heaven before we can understand that there has only ever been one Soul?

It's so blatantly obvious that I want to scream it at you all so you may wake up,

And then I realise I would only be screaming it at myself, for We are One,

Perhaps it bothers me that my brothers have not yet accepted this, because I myself have not yet fully grasped it,

Perhaps the world is still disunited and waging war with itself because I myself am not yet whole and still battling my own demons,

Maybe the universe is still expanding further away from its centre, because I, because we, are still moving further away from that which we are,

That which we were, and that which we wish to become,

But for how much longer will I continue to choose to be what I am not?

For how much longer will we refuse to see what we are? For how many more lifetimes will we continue to move apart?

Have we not already gone far enough? Or perhaps too far? Will we have to again return to the start?

Do you remember the conflict of Atlantis and Lemuria?

XXVIII

A leaf is relieved from the branch of the tree
After a lifetime of service it is finally free
So the breeze decides to ask of the leaf
'Now my friend, where is it you wish to be?'

The leaf replies with a great gasp
'My God, it never occurred to me to ask
To where I would go
Once my time upon the tree had passed'

'I always assumed I would be returned to the lord'
At that point the wind laughed out with a roar
'My dear, for so long I have whispered to you
But you danced your time away, my advices you ignored.'

XXIX

With the tether of duty have you been bound to greatness, lovingly I did tie thy hands in accordance with thy own wish,

And at your hand now awaits an imperative task, the arms of its consequence are reaching both far and wide,

To hold within them the fate of this that you call your world, that the parchment of the next may soon unfurl,

Far too great are the pending implications, for you to resign from this your latest incarnation,

For existence has long been yearning for the peace that your example will bring,

A new age is waiting patiently at the breaking dawn, I urge thee child, let her in,

For she is softly spoken and of few words, she knocks on no door, you must open yourself to her,

Though weary of your earthly fetters you may be, and sore vexed by the machinations of those who call themselves humanity,

Hold firm this life as a child clings to his mother, that you may soon withdraw these lines that divide you from one another,

Remember that you yourself chose this circumstance, that you might fulfill a certain purpose in this lifetime,

The gates of the agreement that you have entered are both grand and weighty,

And to each and every one of you, my children, these gates are opened accordingly,

Equal to your capacity to gratify, a portion is bestowed upon you in this life,

So charge forth bravely O reflection of mine, I assure you that no peace shall you find,
Save within the fulfillment of your obligation,

Not for any judgment that any being may place on your actions, or the course that you may choose to take,
But for the fact that it was with your own blessed self, that this weighty agreement was, in pre-existence, made,

Now the peace of humankind and that of your heart, both equal in significance and intertwined,
Are waiting for you at the finish line that lies beyond time,

The peace you seek will meet you at the completion of the task, with which you have been charged,

So tarry not my Love, for my Love it doth not delay, it is simultaneous and ever-present at all times,

As constant as your very breath and the beat of your heart, so remove idleness from your state of mind,

Banish sloth from your body, seek no more to find those things you believe to have lost to time,
For time, in truth, it does not exist, it exists only within lies,

Grieve not for the past you imagine to have occurred, for it is but the reflection of a mirror,
As you change in the present moment you recreate the past by changing its present significance,
Just as a shadow that follows you wherever you may be, and though it may be dark,
It is you who offer and alter the meaning of the past by the shadow you choose to cast,

So turn your face towards the light, that you may leave this fleeting puppet show behind,

For if you turn away from the light, your shadows will only grow longer and in them you will remain blind,

And as for the future, it does not exist but for in this very moment,

The future is a mirage that is vanquished with every step that you take forward,

It is in the now that the future is born, and in the very same moment it is slain,

The present moment will forevermore stand upon the future's grave,

So hold firm this moment for that is all there has ever been, one single moment of creation,

Upon the script of existence there exists no regretful past, nor any future salvation,

It is only this very moment that can be saved, so breathe your life into it and take from it a breath in return,

That from the ebb and flow of the ocean of life you may learn,

Do not barter your thoughts for pennies, nor give them freely to those in need,

For that will gain you naught but the cost of a fare to the land of poverty,

Instead contain and dwell upon each thought, water it with contemplation that it might grow,

Into a firm oak and that oak into a forest of trees, then furnish your thoughts with the vines of your most vivid dreams,

Let those vines fill the spaces between your forest and that of the rest of the world,

Such that the canopy of that forest may protect you, and its fruits give sustenance to all,

Gather now your thoughts as you would your troops, in the defence of the idealism of youth,

Train the direction of your desires as you would train your archers, for your desires shall direct you towards your fate,

But fear not your destination in any case, for in truth there exists neither honour nor disgrace,

Only the contentment of your heart, which is to be my eternal dwelling place,
And I wish for my home to be one of peace, that we may both rest,

I know that you fear defeat in the face of this your greatest task, and so it is that of you I now ask,

To remind yourself of the infallibility of your cause, for if you fall short of your own expectations, you may return once more,
Or you can continue to return forevermore,

If ever you find yourself under siege, be patient and firm until the day preparedness arrives,

For your cavalry, as capable as they may be, must needs await the proper moment to advance,

Be righteous and fair to others, but just as importantly, you must be so to yourself,
For boundless generosity, when undeserved, is but a sign of one's guilt,

So give of yourself freely my dear, buy only as much as you are willing to receive,
For your Love is only true to the extent that you Love your own being,
And of this I wish for you infinitely,

As a knight upon the field of life, show justice in your movements across these lands,

Seek to slay no unarmed man, nor cease your charge to aid a comrade who be maimed,

Lest ye yourself become acquainted with that same fate, for existence is no matter of life and death, it is merely a game,

Instead consider how your previous actions may have caused your comrade to fall,
And seek to own that action no more,

For there are those who can see to the needs of the fallen, they watch from the spiritual realm,

But entrusted to you is a task only you can complete, and it is for this reason you find yourself at life's helm,

Forget not that to mine eyes all outcomes are victorious, it is only you who believes in the concept of defeat,
So charge forth my brave steed,

Be not bewildered by the sights and sounds of the battlefield of life, let not your heart seize when you meet with strife,

For many a soldier hath paid for a single moment of hesitation, with another lifetime of testing preparation,

Let not the moment pass, for the moment is here and now, waiting for your embrace with open arms,
Atop the hill from which your enemy doth charge, so step forth into the light, my blessed child,

Let not the pain of that which you have seen, deter you from becoming the exalted being you have always been,

And if it so happens that you have enjoyed well-being and a loving upbringing, let not your gratitude turn its face towards guilt,

For each and every one of you crafted your own circumstance in that realm on high, so you could further develop particular skills,

Let not the magnitude of the glory that awaits, overshadow the knowingness of your deserved fate,

For each cup this hand has ever crafted, will be full with my Love to its very brim,
The moment their eyes kiss the light of the day of our reunion,

Some cups though are greater in depth,
And as such, to them is greater my debt,

So shed your Love, my Love, as the clouds shed their tears, cry out loud your call, let your heart no longer harbour fear,
Consider neither who is deserving of such grace, nor how it is that your vessel shall be filled,
The tears of separation you have cried in your moments of longing are, to me, as pure as the blood of the martyr spilt,

The songbirds that sing at day's break, have forever been singing my praises of you,
I have loved you more than you have known and before you ever knew,

These words are but fragile fingers, they can in nowise convey the bravery you did display,
That day you chose to return to the world of physical existence, in remembrance of My Name,

You are my knights in spiritual armour, so bare your naked chest to any enemies that may be,
For the enemy in this spiritual quest you have undertaken, will have naught but uncertainty and doubt as artillery,

Their spears will be constructed of fears, their shields only as steadfast as their faith,

And though they may draw their swords against us, these are but blades of grass when swung upon Our face,

This darkness that seems to surround you at times, brings naught but joy to this heart of mine,

For were it not for the darkness of uncertainty, how could that blessed light of yours shine,

Were I to grant such luminosity to all of creation you would surely have been blinded by its light,

And so it is that in this realm I have separated the day from the night,

That you could arrive at the greatest version of the grandest vision you have had of yourself,

Only after having experienced the darkest night of your soul's plight.

XXX

Move from servitude to certitude

Let your attitude to life, prove your worth to live it

Let the Love you show others, give birth to vivid

Dreams of that which is yet to come

Let your faith meet your knowledge so they can be one

Let the light at end enter the depths of the tunnel

So the signs that are sent become clear to us all

For the breezes that blew

Were the same whisperings of truth

As the seeds we did sow

In the misspent years of our youth

So cry out my dear friends, with the full force of your lungs

Not with the ache of your heart,

Sing to the sky the songs we once sung

Before we were pulled apart

From each other as we came into this world

For you and I were once as one

But now they call us the moon and the sun

XXXI

To where do the understanding go when they themselves need to be understood?

Where do the brave go when they need to cower, and the strong when they need a moment to be weak?

Where do the stoic go when they need to cry? Why do questions taunt me? Why do answers hide?

For who are the clouds shedding their tears? Why is it that rivers must bleed?

Where do the generous go when they have nothing left with which to quench others' insatiable greed?

Where do the consolers of grief go when they themselves feel the need to grieve?

Which direction do leaders turn to when they can no longer bear the responsibility to lead?

From whom does the compass ask for directions? Where do the ocean's waves go when they wish to be still?

From whom do the healers seek healing, when they are sick of the world's ills?

And where do our hopes go when we leave them unfulfilled?

Where does the sun hide at night? Where does the breeze sit when it has no will to move?

What happens to seeds that don't sprout? And what of flowers that never bloom?

Where is it that our hopes and dreams retire to when the time for them has passed?

To where do the steadfast retreat when they no longer have the strength to hold fast?

Where do the forgivers seek solace when they have no compassion left with which to forgive?

Where do the lovers go when they have no Love left to give? And what of the givers of life who have lost the will to live?

Who is transcribing our transgressions? Do we pay for them here or in the hereafter?

And finally, how does the lover return to the beloved when it was he who left her?

XXXII

His name was Nick, he looked dishevelled and disorientated, some would have called him mentally sick,

But I tell you there was nothing wrong with him, he had just witnessed some things you have not yet seen,

He would talk to the clouds and the crowds alike, his fingers were cigarette stained, he drank his coffee strong and hot,

I was sitting at a café, alone, wrapped in the darkness of my own thoughts that day we met,

Some days I want to call just to remind him of how much I Love him, but he has no phone number or any known address,

I remember taking a drag of my cigarette and releasing the smoke into the air,

Watching it, like my hopes and dreams, slowly disappear,

He was walking past, talking almost as fast, when suddenly he stopped and said 'Hey! What are you doing here?'

'How is mum, dad, how are your sisters? Where have you been all these years?'

He asked for a cigarette, so I rolled him one, he put his hand on my shoulder and said 'I've missed you son,'

We shared a brief moment, it lasted an eternity, I looked at him and he smiled back at me,

Then before I knew it he turned and continued his way down the street,

'I'll see you on Sunday,' he called out with a wave of his hand, I whispered back, 'Take care my friend,'

I didn't think much about that strange meeting in the week that passed,

But sure enough, the very next Sunday I walked into a different café, and there he was,

He was sitting at an outside table for two, next to him was an empty chair,

He smiled and nodded for me to sit, not the least bit surprised to have seen me there,

I got him a drink and ordered some food, when I sat back down I asked him 'Nick, who are you?'

'I have been your brother,' he said 'I have been your friend and your enemy,

We have met in many lifetimes and I'm telling you this now because I know you are ready to believe,'

I didn't say much else, I just listened to him speak, frantically and mostly in Greek,

Every time someone walked past he would call out and wave, but they would pretend they didn't see,

'How are you mother?' He called out, 'How are you father? How are you my brother, my sister? How are you my beloved?'

Without fail he would call out to each and every one of them as they walked past,

Each time they ignored him my heart would seize, but he would just laugh,

He laughed out loud hysterically, pointing at them and slapping his knee, before turning back to me to continue muttering in Greek,

Finally, I interrupted him and said 'Nick I don't understand Greek, but I want to understand what it is that you see,

Can you please tell me?'

He looked into my eyes and gazed at my soul,
He said,

'They don't remember, they've all forgotten, but you still remember, you still know,'

He leant across the table and said, 'You remember that place, you remember what we were told,'

Then he whispered, 'We are all One,'

He said,

'We are all One, but those who remember this fact are far too few,

You and I, we chose to come back to this realm that we might remind the others of what they all once knew,

I've scattered my mind somewhere along the line in this game called time, so no one believes what I have to say,

But you still have your mind, and so I've come to help you along your way,

I will come to you in your times of greatest need, I will give you clues whenever you are ready to hear,

So take these pieces of my mind that I have left, pass them to others, have no fear,

And though this game called life seems to never end, live with peace my dear friend,

For it will all be over in the blink of an eye and in the realm of spirit we will be together again,'

Thank You Nicholas,
I will see you soon.

XXXIII

Existence is not really reality, it is actually no more than an analogy,

Creation was a question that was asked, and life, well life is the answer to the question,

You see, I used to ask myself 'Who does this God think he is?'

To bring me to life without asking me if I even want to exist,

To live and then die, only to go to eternal heaven or the fires of perpetual hell,

To love me, create me, then judge me on what I did badly and what I did well?

Either way I'm stuck in an eternal existence from which there is no escape, constantly swaying between love and hate,

And if I'm lucky enough to be a Buddhist, then I'll be reborn into a world from which there is also no escape!

That's a pretty sadistic God if you ask me, I suppose that's why they refer to God as a he and not a she,

Because only a man could think of such a torturous never-ending prank,

I can just imagine him laughing out loud as he leaves us to ourselves to go and have another...

And if it so happens that one of these poor fools has had enough one day and he loses his cool,

And shouts out 'To hell with you God and I'll see you there, I've had enough of this!'

Then he will end up with a psychiatrist who doesn't know her shiz from her nit,

She'll pretend to listen as she prescribes you medications to numb your brain,

Then send you home so you can try to explain to your wife who also happens to be a psych, that apparently the man she married is clinically insane,

Well that's not the kind of God I believe in anymore, because a part of me tells me I've been here once or twice before,

But it was only after I was separated and divorced from the aforementioned wife,

That I was forced to sit in the silent darkness of my cave to unravel the paradoxes of life,

Somewhere along the line, between the time I escaped the solitary confines of my mind and my re-arrest and institutionalisation,

I stumbled across a rather profound realisation,

It occurred to me, that there could not possibly be a way to address a question to a particular entity,

If he or she did not already exist,

How could I have been asked the question 'do you wish to exist?' if I wasn't already there to listen to it?

So you see, instead of experiencing reality, we now find ourselves in a well-constructed analogy,

Which closely resembles the true nature of our existence, and in effect we were asked the question,

'What do you want to be?'

But in actuality if you read the fine print you will clearly see,

*Note to self – there can be no distinction made between the terms I, you, me or We, and henceforth these terms can be interchanged within any context of this gleaning, without influencing the outcome or intended meaning.

So in fact, the question that was asked was,
'What am I, and what do I wish to be?'

The answer to this question cannot be right or wrong, it cannot be given a grade, rank or class,

Your answer cannot be given a percentage score on a sliding scale, nor marked fail or pass,

It was an open-ended question that you asked yourself, so you can respond to it however you want,

Short answer, multiple choice or an oral presentation, written essay, musical composition or abstract representation,

A video response, a classical dance piece or a theatre performance on stage,

An epic novel, a finger painting exhibition or just a dot in the middle of the page,

Because you asked the question 'What am I, and what do I wish to be?' And the life you choose to live is the answer that creates your reality,

You asked yourself the question 'What am I, and what do I wish to Be' and your life is your answer,

Which means we are all valedictorians, and God is an atheist, transvestite, interpretive dancer.

XXXIV

Where are you Love?

Are you alone when you leave me?

Do you have a place to call home when I fill my heart with fear and hate?

Where do you hide when this world leaves no place for one such as you?

Do the clouds keep you company? Do you fly with the birds as they wing their way home?

Do you cry when your call is not heard? Do you feel forgotten? Are you ever forlorn?

Or do you smile while you wait for us to turn back to you? I miss you when you are gone,

But when you do leave me, I know it is of my own fault,

Something that I've said or done, perhaps something I've forgotten.

XXXV

Her name was Aryan, she was pure of heart, sweet of tongue
and light of skin,

Eyes the shape of the earth and the colour of the sky, there was
a universe within,

Taller than the tallest of trees and yet as humble as the soil
beneath its roots,

She is five thousand years old now, and still none can rival the
fortitude of her youth,

For the children of Aryan have been asked to bear much for the
sake of humanity,

Scattered across this earth, they were once the bearers of the
banner of unity,

But her people are now exiled, executed and downtrodden,
suffering generations of repression,

Those left behind seek the comfort of the needle's touch to
alleviate the darkness of their depression,

Her hair now bloodstained white was once jet black and waist
long, but she has been raped and laid to waste for far too long,

Behind closed curtains she is tormented by foreign invaders,
external puppeteers of false internal saviors,

For centuries Aryan gave birth to poets, philosophers and
mathematicians,

Lovers, mystics, astrologers and architects of an ever-advancing
civilisation,

When she stretched the wings of her empire Aryan conquered
no one,

But simply invited them to enter the protection of her loving
home,

Christians, Hindus and Jews alike were comforted and
protected in her open arms,

No one was forced to change his or her language, culture or religion,

And of religions her's was that of Zartosht, or as you know him Zoroaster,

It was his spiritual principles that guided her people, and Aryan's faithful prayed to the sun God Mazda,

The pen of her son Cyrus, scripted the very first charter of human rights,

Two and a half thousand years ago he told us that we were all equals in the eyes of God,

Even before the Son of God walked upon this earth, His humble servant Cyrus, son of Aryan,

Gathered and protected followers of all faiths into the safety of his prosperous lands,

For he knew that they were all one,

When Jerusalem was besieged by Nebuchadnezzar of Babylon, the people of Moses were given safety in the land of Aryan,

With her patronage, protection and blessings, the Jewish people returned to rebuild their temples in Jerusalem,

How have you forgotten the magnanimity of Aryan O children of Israel?

That Austrian who martyred so many of your brethren was no child of Aryan, but a bastard child of her deserters,

And Aryan, O how she wailed to the heavens for forgiveness upon hearing he had called himself of her,

When Nabonidus of Babylon tried to cover the sun with the moon,

His own people invited the king of Aryan to save them from that fool,

Aryan never enslaved like the Egyptians, she never burnt libraries like the Greeks,

Aryan never sought to abolish the faith of the pagans as the Romans did, to replace them with cobblestone streets,

It was Constantine who desecrated Jerusalem in the name of the Son of God,

He was the one who exiled the Jews and built churches on top of their Synagogues,

It was Omar the Muslim who recaptured Jerusalem, and Saladin who invited the Jewish people back,

It was the followers of the Son of God who exiled and slaughtered you, how could you have forgotten that?

It was Einstein, one of the greatest minds of our time, a stateless exile of Israel, who once advised,

If we treat the Palestinians as a coloniser would, then we have learnt nothing in all these years of exile,

Aryan never had to Love others as though they were her children, for in her eyes there existed no distinction,

And speaking of children, while the Spartans were snuffing the lives of their newborns,

Implementing incestuous laws of military breeding, in order to create a race of warriors to suppress the discontent of their slaves,

The children of Aryan were following the teachings of Zoroaster to the advent of a brighter day,

They walked slowly and assuredly towards the abandonment of prejudice, persecution and slavery,

Established the equality of men and women as law, while the rest of the world still lived in savagery,

Depict her how you wish in your textbooks and stories, O ye of small minds,

For Aryan has proven her graciousness to the world time after time after time,

Speaking of textbooks, Avicenna's name was actually pronounced Ibn Sina, he wrote the Canon of Medicine,

In a time when the people of Britain had only just learnt to jump Hadrian's fence,

One thousand years ago he wrote that text, at the time of the fall of Rome,

Until the 16th century that book stood out alone, as the most advanced medical text humankind had ever known,

Aryan's poets wrote Europe's textbooks on mathematics, physics and astrology,

Omar Khayyam, portrayed by the west as a drunkard poet, wrote the theory of non-Euclidean geometry,

So far ahead of the available technology that it could not be proven for 750 years,

In 1952 the people of Aryan had selected,
A president who was democratically elected,

But when his ideas took a life of their own,
And he wished to increase the price of their oil,

The United States of America,
Openly staged a coup d'état,

They ousted him and in his place they placed their own puppet the Shah,

When he managed to find a mind of his own they covertly staged another coup d'état,

Even after all that has been done to the people of the world, the children of Aryan hold nothing against the United States,

They just want to put a stop to the raping of their mother,
Our mother,
Earth,

The United States is in possession of more armed nuclear weapons than the rest of the world combined,

Is there no one else who is wondering why?

The US armed and trained the Taliban in the first place, to fight socialists across the border,

It is because of our lust for resources that so many families are displaced and slaughtered,

Africa's land is so fertile for all the blood she has been asked to shed,

Our cars get bigger, our minds get thicker as we continue to dance upon the graves of our dead,

So to those who wish to incite hatred and cause more bloodshed, you should know that my pen is now aimed at your head,

Because in the last one hundred years humanity has caused itself more death, destruction and suffering,

Than the rest of human history combined, all the way back to the beginning,

And if we do not soon cease our warmongering ways and provocations,

Our resource based conflicts, manufactured revolutions and incitations,

So the so-called developed world may supply both sides of the conflict with arms,

Than we will wipe out our civilisation as we have done before, do you remember Atlantis and Lemuria?

If only we could stretch our memories as far back as we stretch our slingshots,

We'd remember that the oldest stones of the Egyptian pyramids are actually at the top,

And that we, the inhabitants of earth, are all descendants of David, I am one of their rocks,

I tell you now, if we were to take just one breath in unison this entire system of hate would collapse,

So come at me, O tyrants of the lands, I will show you how I can fly,

I will hurl these verses at you like David's rock through Goliath's third eye,

Come at me if you dare, for I am a child of the land of Aryan, a descendent of the people of Lemuria,

I light fires with my tongue,
In the hearts of men,
    As a Celt I slayed dragons,
With a motion of my pen,
    As an Inca I welcomed the Olmecs onto this earth,
I have bent my mind so far back I remember the birth of the universe,

    Because I was there, and so were you all,
    But some have forgotten that blessed morn we sat beneath the
Tree of Lote, so I've returned to remind you once more,
    That we are in fact one entity, and we share one soul.

I asked if I could walk beside her
    And she said 'No,
That is where the breeze will blow'

I asked if I could walk on the other side
    And she said 'No,
That is where the sun will hide'

I asked if I could walk in front of her
    And she said 'No,
You know not yet where to go'

I asked if could walk behind her
    And she said 'No,
That is where my dust will fall'

'Then what shall I do'
    I asked,
'O Queen of my heart'

    Wait for the breeze to stand still and the sun to rest,
Let the dust settle behind me once I have left,

    Then seek me in the silent stillness of the darkness,
For that is where your light will shine the brightest,

    And if your Love be true and your ardour strong,
You will find your way back to that place we once called home.

XXXVII

Patiently has the light of truth been waiting for the moment it may caress your face,

Yet curtains of fear you have drawn, with closed windows and locked your doors,

You dwell in slumber upon your couch, refusing to awake you lock the world out,

In the dark corners of your chambers you sit, claiming this world to be void of significance,

While just beyond the closed doors of your mind's eye await my fields of celestial bliss,

You doubt your own ability to Love, so you create stories of a vengeful creator,

Questioning the existence of unconditional Love, you continue to find reason to hate more,

You offer one hand to doubt and the other to fear, and let them lead you further astray,

You heed their mischievous whisperings and of their desires you find reason to pray,

Save my soul, save my child, save me from myself and my evil desires,

With these empty words you fall to your knees, that within my heart you may find my mercy,

And so it is that you continue to break my heart, causing me grief in believing we were ever apart,

You call one entity the light and the other you title the sun, how can these two ever be anything but one?

You claim the rain is not the cloud and the river separate from the sea,
But how can the waves and the ocean be separated? How can I exist without thee?

We are one and the same, the desert is no greater than the single grain of sand,
And no finger can will grasp the pen until it recognises its oneness with the hand,

So turn now to your brothers and your sisters and together say aloud 'We are God and God is One,'

That you may find yourself in that place where the earth no longer turns her back to the sun.

XXXVIII

I know you fear being alone, I know you fear the sound of your own silence,

And so you interrupt her and fill her with sounds that are void of sense,

Your idle talk and your constant chatter are but ways you keep the silence at bay,

You suppress your emotions with inconsequential motions, for you fear what your emotions might have to say,

You busy yourselves with thoughtless words and with baseless thoughts,

You read of one another's lives, bicker and backbite, talk about your mindless work,

And then, you occupy your spare time with that sanctioned savagery you call sport,

That even in your idlest of moments you can suppress any meaningful thought,

I know you feel alone, for I too feel the same,

Surrounded by those who Love us the most, still we battle to defend our hearts of the pain,

The pain of our separation,

We grieve the death of our friends and family, not for where they have gone,

But for the fact that we fear having to one day take that very same journey alone,

We fear death as though it were an end, a separation from the world of being,

But life and death are not separate entities, rather the ebb and flow of the one same ocean,

The changing of seasons from winter to spring,

In the company of those who Love us the most, sometimes we can feel the most alone,

For they are the ones who know us the best, and yet our relationships even with them are not whole,

If we feel a sense of separation from those closest to us, how much further away must we feel from the other parts of Us,

And that is what scares us the most,

If my father and I still don't see eye to eye, if my brothers' actions cause my mothers to cry,

If my siblings continue to fuss and fight, if there is even a chance my lover might,

One day misplace her Love for me, then what hope is there for the rest of humanity,

And that is what scares us the most,

When we don't take the time to smile at a stranger as they walk past, we give ourselves reason to fear walking alone in the dark,

If I don't stop to help a student who has scattered his books, and I leave him alone to deal with the sly grins and gleeful looks,

Then to whom am I calling when I cry myself to sleep, even if an omnipotent God were to exist,

I would have broken his heart earlier that day, for I let God collect his own books as I went on my way,

And that is what scares me the most.

XXXIX

I see dead people, and I see them everywhere, hiding in dark spaces and walking in the light of day,

I see dead people, but they think they are still alive,
If you watch closely you will see them being gently crushed by the weightless insignificance of their lives,

Some of them aren't dead yet, they are slowly drowning in an ocean of lies, and still they continue to water it,

I see dead people rolling along in metal coffins, their faces are blank and bare,
They make their way from distant places towards their concrete high-rise graves, and from there,
They plan and plot the deaths of those who have escaped their destitute state of affairs,

These walking dead will not stop working until every last one of us is amongst the dead,
They work tirelessly to find ever more efficient ways of creating from life, a living death,

I tell you now if you ever happen to talk to one, endeavor to refrain from direct eye contact,
Because they can suck the life out of any living being without breaking a sweat,

But don't worry too much, they usually don't talk much, even in the café queue, on the bus or the train,
These dead people numb themselves with tablets and tabloids, propaganda spreadsheets and iPhone games,
For though they can drain the life out of those still living, if these dead people happen to look each other in the eye,
They will spontaneously combust from the recognition of the lie they call a life,

The manufacturing plant that creates these walking dead starts with a capital, and it all ends with a schism,

The rupture of mind, body and soul is what creates dead people from the living,

Because this system is not for the common in us, it is about survival and physical fitness,

Regardless of spiritual health, but what these dead people have forgotten is that there is actually only one of Us,

And they are the limbs that are showing signs of rot.

XL

I remember the days I used to wake up excited to be alive,
bursting to leave the house to greet the day that had just arrived,
Because I was in Love,

I would wake up before my parents and sneak into the laundry,
smiling to myself I'd carry the iron back to my bedroom quietly,

As a four-year-old I taught myself to iron my shirts and my
shorts, even my underwear and socks,
Everything had to be perfect, because I was in Love,

I knew I was in Love even though I had not yet learnt how to
spell the word,
I'd only just learnt how to spell my own name, for some reason
I wrote the letter R backwards in those days,

It's been twenty-five years since I've seen her, but I'll never
forget how her smile would make me feel,
I may have only been four years old back then, but I know what
I felt for her was real,

I would rush to get ready for school each day so I could wait
for her by the gate,
But my parents were wogs fresh off the boat, which meant I
was always late,

I would sit at the back of the room and let my thoughts run
wild in her waist long hair,
Waiting for the graceful motion of her delicate hands placing a
stray strand behind her ear,
Hoping that if I stared for long enough she might look back, I
can't remember her name but I know her hair was black,

Or maybe it was brown, I'm not quite sure, when our teacher
would read to us she would let us sit on the floor,

I would never sit next to her because I was too shy,

I'd sit close enough to feed my Love, but never brave enough to look her in the eye,

One day we were drawing at the art table, and she couldn't find a pencil the colour red,

My heart stumbled and my hands fumbled as I offered her mine, but she took the one from the boy next to me instead,

I was as heartbroken as I have ever been in my life, I swear I almost burst into tears right there and then,

I looked down at my pencil to realise she hadn't taken it from me because I'd chewed the end again,

Isn't it strange how some memories fade away while others never seem to leave our minds?

No matter how hard we push them away, they always come back time after time,

Sometimes I wonder if I hadn't chewed that pencil, and if she had taken it from my hand,

Would we have ended up together as I had planned?

Would she have become my wife, would we have built a house together and had three kids?

And then I realise that if she had taken that pencil from me that day, and said yes to my proposal at recess,

Then I would never have written this.

XLI

He was only ten,

He was too young to understand what it meant, to work two jobs and study, while trying to raise a family and keep up with the rent,

Because he was only ten,

He was old enough to have ever-growing wants and needs and expectations,

Old enough to know that he didn't fit in at school, and how to spell the word 'Immigration,'

But not quite old enough to recognise the silent grief of a father struggling to breathe,

A man who was imprisoned at the age of seventeen for expressing his egalitarian beliefs,

Then spent the rest of his life an exile, a migrant, a greasy wog, Persian refugee,

This boy was just a kid who thought his father was a king with the world at his feet,

Little did he know of his father's sleepless nights as he struggled to resist defeat,

A man whose universal orbit was his wife and three kids, not once did he raise his hands on them no matter what they did,

Instead he would work with every ounce of his being to give them whatever they would want,

Never stopping to ask himself whether they deserved it or not,

This boy was oblivious to the weight already resting on his father's shoulders,

As he watched him give his sisters piggyback rides like an unwavering soldier,

In 1984, with an empty suitcase, a wife and a one-year-old son, he came to this country and decided he'd be stopped by no one,

Not even that university lecturer who pointed him out to a theatre full of students,

Saying 'What will this man ever make of himself? Why are we taking in these useless immigrants?'

His broken English left him unable to come up with a response on the spot,

But that one-year-old son is now a grown man, his mouth's a canon's barrel, and the pen in his hand is a loaded glock,

You see that camel rider you taunted that day, somehow managed to raise a squid,

He's educated, eloquent, well versed and he's got some ink to spit,

He's lyrically armed with philosophical napalm and refuses to be calm, so if I was you I'd raise the alarm because he's about to do some harm,

To any narrow-minded ideologies that may come his way,

You see, I am the proud son of that greasy wog, and I am happy to say,

That I'm an illegitimate immigrant, trying to shed a little bit of light on the plight of the Indigenous,

So listen to this, as you sailed the seven seas, you failed to see, the land you landed on didn't belong to you, or me,

It belonged to the Indigenous custodians, the traditional land-owners, the ones you killed and slaughtered and labelled as the fauna,

You see before you merrily row, row, rowed your boat down the stream, colonising everything that you'd see,

This place you now call Australia was once the land of the dream,

And Dad, there is something that I want you to know that I've never said out loud,

And that is, you are my guiding light, my shelter in the storm, and that of you I am proud,

You might not know this, but I remember what happened that day when I was ten,

I didn't understand the significance of it at the time because I was only a child back then,

But do you remember that day in McDonalds in Cairns, when the girls and I came with you on your work trip,

Sep, Raf and I ate our McMuffin meals and pancakes, while you would just sip on the tea that you brought from home,

I remember you checked the receipt and asked 'Is it possible for one man to say that he ate all of this?'

I thought you were just curious, so I replied 'Sure if he's fat grommet,'

Then kept eating my food as you worriedly folded the receipt and put it back in your wallet,

I didn't realise it then, but I know now why you didn't eat breakfast that day,

You skipped that meal because you didn't actually have enough money to pay,

Your office had told you to justify every cent that you'd spent, so you had to keep the receipt to get your fifty-dollar reimbursement,

You couldn't actually afford to take your three kids with you from Townsville to Cairns,

But when we begged you to take us you did anyway, because you were a selfless man,

I still remember those days you would go from the office to the restaurant, and work non-stop,

And in the dead of night you'd ride your pushbike home to finish your PhD on the injustice faced by the Indigenous mob,

Not once did you let us feel an ounce of your fears or even a fragrance of your pain,

Instead, on your way home you would shed your tears in the rain,

That skipped meal and all the other days that you would hold your silent fast,

Just to put us through school and buy us birthday gifts might now be in the past,

But sometimes I still think of those days,

Because it's those memories that spur me on to write my story, speak my mind and create my art,

Each and every one of your silent sacrifices have played their part,

In creating the man that now stands before you, it is to you that I owe my potentialities too,

You see, that meal you skipped that day for not having had enough money to pay,

Has paved the way for me to now write the book that will save the world one day.

XLII

'Hold me,' she gasped,
And I did as I said 'I'll never let you go,'

If only I could have known how all those years of hurt had
corroded the walls of her heart, I might have been more careful with
mine,
But instead I held unto her like she was a second chance at life,

I wrapped my arms around her body trying to encompass all of
her pain,
Hoping that if I squeezed tightly enough it would seep into my
veins,
But she held me like the ocean's winds holding the ship's mast,
tight and strong,
But as she held me she was pushing us apart, she was pushing
me along,

She was not ready to Love, she was not ready to trust, she was
not yet ready to believe, in us,

She closed her eyes and she sighed long, I took a deep breath to
inhale her grief into my lungs,
Then I kissed her eyes that I might relieve her of all she had
seen in her life,

That night I spent with her I felt I was at home, she made sense
of my past and gave me the strength I needed to go on,
She answered all of the questions of my soul without having
said a word,
I thought to myself that if all I had been through was to meet
her,
Then it was worth it,

That night I learnt of a Love I had never known, I fell so deep and far, so hard and fast, my Love for her took me to a place I had never gone,

And I'm still trying to understand where it all went wrong,

She fell asleep in my arms that night, I lay awake and watched her sleep for a while,

Silently I thanked God, the sun and the moon, I thanked her parents for the way they had raised her,

I thanked the birds that fly and those who don't, I closed my eyes and thanked the universe,

She slept peacefully in my arms that night as I inhaled the fragrance of the nave of her neck,

Softly I kissed her shoulder a few times as I let go of a lifetime's regrets,

Eventually I fell asleep in her arms with my face wrapped in her jet-black hair,

Long and dark, like the years that had passed before I met her,

Her skin was light but her heart was heavy,

Her words was softly spoken but from the way her voice trembled I should have known she was not yet ready,

To fall in Love,

To her I was just a shelter in the storm, somewhere safe to rest for the night, when I woke up the next morning she was already gone,

Her body was still lying next to me, but her sweet skin had turned cold,

Her heart still beat strong but she would not look me in the eye, afraid to let me back into her soul,

Her words were lifeless and she didn't even look back as she said 'The door's unlocked, you can let yourself out,'

It has been two years since that night I held her in my arms, and I still haven't let go,

It has been two years since that morning, and I still haven't given up hope,

The memory of that blessed night has been emblazoned on my mind,

I laid bare for her the naked truth of my Love, and in doing so I ended up blind,

Because I didn't know as I watched over her that night, that she was just an eclipse,

If I had known I would not have stared at her the way I did,

I would have closed my eyes, I knew I should have just walked on by,

If I had known her lips were poison laced, I would not have asked for a taste of her sweet scented lies,

But I didn't know, and so I tripped, I stumbled and I fell in Love with her,

And in doing so I drowned myself,

I drowned in the fuel of my Love and with that look in her eye she lit the spark,

Happily I let myself burn, because with her I felt that I was finally at home,

And now with the ink of my ashes I write these words, that I may recite them in the dark of night,

Hoping she may one day hear the echo of voice, and perhaps come back to me in time.

12. 12. 71.

XLIII

Last night I watched an old man clasping firmly to the hand of his middle-aged son,

He held it so tight it were as if they were One,

Both of their hands were tired and weathered, leathered by a lifetime of tests,

Yet still capable of holding that blessed moment of beauty that I witnessed,

Neither of the men looked at the other, the old man watched his granddaughter dance, the son glanced over at his mother,

The young girl squealed in delight as she spun to the tune of the music,

Her right hand raised to the air, the other holding the edge of her tunic,

The beat became feverish as the air it did fill, the girl spun faster and faster, the two men sat perfectly still,

The young dancer showered her Love on all who watched, as if throwing seeds into the air,

Landing them in the hearts of those mesmerised by her spinning wheel of hair,

These two men, their smiles were subtle, almost imperceptible to the naked eye,

But I saw in the stillness within them, a joy I could not deny,

Two battle-hardened soldiers, each having served a lifetime of life,

Still able to hold the hand of the other as though he were his wife,

There is so much we can convey with words, yet sometimes without them we can say so much more,

I struggled to suppress a few tears as I thought of how much I loved them all,

Though years may pass before father and son might share a loving word,

I was forever changed that night by the silent dialogue I heard,

A dialogue that words could never imagine to express, a Love so deep it left nothing else to be said,

The colour of the old man's beard was fading, but his heart, it shone bright,

His staggered wrinkles straightening the slightest to express his heartfelt delight,

With all of the tears his children had caused to pass beside the bridge of his nose,

His Love had not once given sway, and no matter how far his children would happen to stray,

From the desires of his heart, or how long they might have been apart, his Love still held strong,

And upon their return they always knew that it was to his heart that they would forever belong.

XLIV

My words take me apart piece-by-piece, as they flow out into the air,

Drifting away with the same breeze that once blew through her sweet-scented hair,

So I keep scribing these words, filling these lines, slowly reverse engineering myself,

Trying to find out what I truly am, before I run out of time,

You see, I've been here a few times before and each time I've understood a little bit more,

But I have also created much pain and suffering each time I have come back into this existence,

I've initiated revolutions and hosted tyrannies, I've been the overbearing system and I've led the resistance,

So this time I'm trying to leave behind nothing, or at least become nothing so I no longer have to feel,

But the voices in my dreams tell me that nothing can escape from pain, for pain is what makes Love real,

So I said, 'If nothing can escape pain, then let me be nothing so I can escape it too,'

'If you so wish,' came the reply, 'but remember nothing can be you,'

'Why would nothing want to be me?' I ask, 'I am a ball of contradictions, shortcomings and confused identities and of these things nothing is free,'

That is when I realised I'd stumbled across something truly profound, the answer to one of life's greatest secrets I had unwittingly found,

From contradiction, flux and paradox nothing is free, not sunlight or water nor grace, justice, knowledge or even uncertainty,

The wave trembles as it travels from sun to earth, water transforms from mist to liquid to solid, so on and so forth,

Knowledge is only knowledge for so long as it's true, eventually we disprove it and for it we have no use,

Love comes and goes, is born, then dies, Love is always true, expect for when it's a lie,

A bird flies, then dies, it becomes one with the earth, that earth becomes part of a tree, that tree grows in perfect unity,

And then, the water that has already transformed many times, gives to that tree the very essence of life,

That tree soon gives fruit, the sunlight imparts to that fruit its energy,

That fruit is eaten by something that calls itself a man, someone like me,

Still that man somehow believes, that from the rest of the universe he is separate and free,

So he goes out and kills everything that gives him life, betrays his family, his friends, his parents and his wife,

Then he asks, 'Why life is so cruel, why is the universe so unkind,'

Failing to recognise that it was he who was blind.

XLV

I was the ocean and she was the sea, but in our haste to find each other we did not realise that I was searching for her and she was looking for me,

I looked into the open sky, while she plunged into the depths of her soul, if only we knew,

That we were swaying to the pull of the moon and under the influence of the winds that blew,

If only I could have known that the one I was searching for, was searching for me too,

All that was needed was for me to be still, my waves to cease their sway,

For the ocean and the sea to become the lake, for the rivers to no longer have to pray,

By sacrificing all they had to give, to stop dying and simply live,

Wherever we go, there we will be, but it is only when we stop searching that we finally see,

All we ever wanted we already possessed, we were kings and queens once, we ourselves decided to be dispossessed,

Of our kingdoms and of our lands, we took the crowns off our heads and removed the rings from our hands,

We chose to start over again with nothing to our names, we chose to replace our knowingness with vague dreams,

So we could understand what we once knew with greater depth, so we could become oceans with greater breath,

Our arrogance wished to be humble and our thoughts wished to be read,

Our dreams wanted to become reality and our reality wished to never end,

And so our souls chose to enter bodies that our ideals could be lived,

Our knowledge wished to be experienced so that our faith could become belief,

So we separated again from the One that we loved, we said goodbye in the realm above,

Promising to find each other again in the world of body and mind,

Just to test our Love and strengthen our hearts until the day that we find,

Each other again in this new form, the ship left the port to face the storm,

In search of the beloved's home,

On a quest to find the True Lover, a journey that must be taken alone.

XLVI

You smiled today, and you actually meant it,

You weren't even smiling at me but your joy was so vivid the hairs on my arms, they felt it,
They stood up to feel the warmth of your smile, even time itself stood still for a while,

I don't know your name, you'll probably never know mine, we'll most likely never see each other again,
But that moment of beauty you shared with the world, will forever be emblazoned on my mind my dear friend,

So thank you for your smile and the joy of your heart,
Thank you for the beauty of the eyes with which you look at this world, thank you for doing your part,
In making this glorious existence a little more glorious to live, thank you for giving so generously of the Love you have to give,

I wanted to approach you, to take both your hands in mine,
I wanted to place my head at your feet, I wanted to leave them there for a while,

But then I realised I need not own the beauty in this world for it to be true,
I just need to clear my heart and cleanse my eyes, that I may see in everything, the same beauty I witnessed in you,

Just the fact that you exist is enough solace for me, so I will learn to Love you as the mountain loves the sea,

From afar and kept apart, the mountain continues to catch the rains that fall,
Just as I catch these words as they fall onto my page once more,

And just as the mountains guide the waters to the river, and the rivers to the sea,

So too to will I sing your praise until the ends of my days, offering to others the joy you gave me,

I will give these words to the world, just as you gave us your smile,

So I may fill the hearts of others with the same joy with which you filled this heart of mine.

XLVII

Tell me what to do my dear music, tell me what to do before I lose it,

Tell me there is reason and purpose behind the motion of the universe, let me know that the struggle for true Love is worth it,

Let the next song I hear give me a new idea or at least offer another clue,

Let the notes carry me away to that place where the boundaries are blurred between us two,

Bring words to life, let them dance in that place beyond space and time,

Bring to me melodies that will remind me the universe has a soul, and that its soul is mine,

Bring images to the eye of my mind, of truths that I have not yet seen,

Give me directions to places I have not yet been,

Make clear to me O music, the secrets of the universe that I did once know,

Remind me of the scent of the one I once held close,

Come to me my dear music, bring with you your paintbrush and your paints,

Bring me to life in the dead of night, make my mind your canvas, let us create,

Let us unravel the possibilities that could be, and those that once were,

Take me to that place where I can once again be with her.

XLVIII

The seed and the drop of water crossed paths one day, they got to discussing the nature of God,

The seed proclaimed that God was the earth for it was the earth that gave protection, nutrition and the opportunity for her to spring forth with fruits and blossoms,

It was the earth that allowed the seed to become the tree, it was the earth that held firm the tree's roots as the winds of perdition did blow, and it was to the earth that all of her life's efforts would return,

The drop of water was outraged, protesting that it was obvious God was the ocean, for it was from the ocean that she came, and it was to the ocean that she would return,

It was the ocean that gave birth to the cloud and sent the drop to the mountain's top, to start its journey back to the ocean,

In its attempt to convince the seed that God was the ocean, the drop of water argued that without the ocean the earth would become the desert,

The seed retorted, 'Never, for the desert is the devil,' the drop of water laughed out saying 'Ah, at last we have found the point of our agreeance,'

So though the seed and the drop assigned their faith to different Gods, they both saw the desert as the devil,
With that they agreed to leave the other to worship a false God and went on their way,

Then came the day the seed came across the grain of sand,

From that day forth Jerusalem has wept tears of blood,

To the drop of water, the desert is the devil, the seed is the infidel and the ocean is God,

To the grain of sand, the ocean is the devil, the seed is the infidel and the desert is God,

To the seed, the desert is the devil, the drop of water the infidel and the earth is God,

And God, O how She wails into the winds that blow across her face, and God, O how He weeps as the clouds do break,

For God, She sees the pieces of herself in conflict with each other, in search of His blessed beauty,

And God, He weeps for the pain they cause each other, in the name of Her Love,

While God continues to cut itself up into smaller pieces, trying to understand itself.

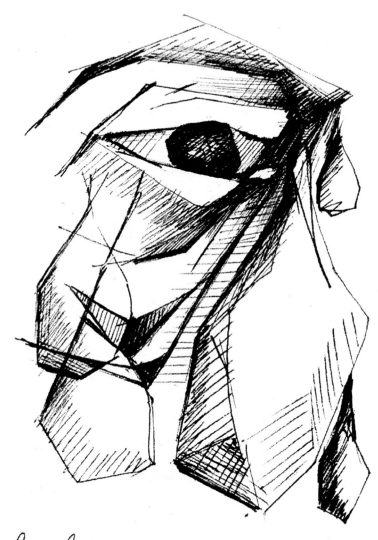

L Daliu

XLIX

When I see you I see perfection,

I see a being of light brought to life through Love,

I see a reflection,

Of myself,

I see God,

Resting in the corners of your mouth as you point them towards the sky,

Why don't you smile more often child? Why don't you smile?

If only you could see the beauty of the soul I see when I look into your eyes,

In your breath is the vastness of the universe and all of its skies,

And God,
She swims in your tears as they run down your face,

And God,
He loves the sound that your heartfelt laughter makes,

For God,
She is the breeze that dances with your hair,

And God
He is the rain that washes away all of your cares,

So let your hair out my Love, let me watch it dance with the wind, look with joy to the clouds that watch from us above,

Imagine the beauty they see, if only for a moment, won't you turn your face to me?

For my heart, it aches for you, I know that all you've ever wanted was to be wanted, and I tell you now that you are,

So much more than you think you are, you are the wish that someone has placed upon a star,

And one day you will find that person,
It might just be me,

For now just remember that you are loved and adored, you are missed even when you are near,

And God, She has never been far, He is looking at you every time you turn your face to the mirror,
Clear yourself of your fears and you will see life a little clearer,

With every fear you manage to overcome your heart expands a bit more,
And it's able to carry a little more Love, until it can fit the entirety of the world,

And when you can do that, you will realise that this was all you,

It was all Us,

We did this,

We created this universe just for fun.

L

I could not see myself for that which I truly was, for I was, all that was,

I could not witness myself from outside of myself, for I encompassed all that was,

I could not investigate, understand or comprehend what I was, for at whatever point at which I stood I was still within myself,

I knew of Love, yet I could not experience what it was to Love, I was Love, but could not know what it was to be Loved,

For I was, all that was,

I could not experience justice, grace, forgiveness, joy or delight, I could not experience honour, humility, courage, kindliness or sacrifice,

For I was, all that was,

I could not feel what it was to forgive or to be forgiven, for there was none to forgive,

I could not be humble or humiliated, for there was none to serve with humility,

I could not be kind or be shown kindness, for there existed naught but The Self,

I could not know what it was to be honourable or to be dishonoured, for there was none to honour,

So, for the purpose of experiencing myself, to embody what I could only imagine, and to experience becoming what I already was,

I decided to separate the inseparable, and dismember the entangled,

As with the atom that was split, I too decided to separate myself from myself,

Unleashing a universe of energy, propelling myself into every direction imaginable, and unimaginable,

And in doing so, I brought existence into being,

In that moment of creation, with that decision to initiate the separation, with full knowledge, and of mine own doing,

I relinquished my powers, and distributed them, evenly and equally throughout the universe,

In the hope that I would once again find them and understand them with greater depth,

And with them, recreate the universe once again,

Having once possessed the powers of creation, I knew that I would find them again,

But rather than having owned them, I would have learned and earned them,

I did not create you in my image or likeness, for that would be analogous and empty, like a shadow, lifeless and inanimate, rather, you and I are as one, I created you by destroying myself,

Through selflessness I created what you now know as the self, by choosing to become nothingness, I became everything,

By separating myself from myself, I became the universe,

Wanting to know what I was, I separated myself so that I could create and become you,

But now the time has come for you to remember yourself, so We can become Me,

What I decided to separate in order to become you, you must now re-member in order to become Me,

It was out of my Love for you that I created you, now out of your Love for Me, you must recreate Me,

Do not forget me, for when you forget me you forget yourself, and when you forget yourself you forget what you were,

When you forget what you were, you fail to recognise what you have always been,

And that my Beloved Friend,

Is God,

For You am I,

We are God,

And God is One.

LI

My mind it tends to wander,
I follow it to places that I have never been,
We walk hand in hand and in the dark and we search,
For what the light of day has not yet seen,

We go as far as I dare,
Before we stand, silent in the stillness,
My mind is my guide,
And I, just a humble witness,

The lowly scribe that must describe,
How we arrived at such a place,
With no more than a pen in my hand,
I attempt to draw images of God's face,

So as we enter the depths of the woods,
I lay these words across the page, as best I can,
Rather than leave myself a trail of bread,
My mind finds its way home by following my hand,

For without these words I would wonder hopelessly,
Forever across the waters of this infinite sea,
Upon which we roam,
Never quite sure where to go ashore,
Or upon which land to make my home.

LII

There was once a time when rain had not yet fallen on this earth, and there were no oceans across her face, a time beyond our recollection but not our imagination.

At what point did that first droplet land upon the earth? When did the very first wave of water travel across the ocean to make its way from one shore to another?

Did that first droplet realise the significance of its actions as it carried its silent message? Was it conscious of its own existence?

When will the waves that lap at the beach, begin to comprehend their relationship with the moon?

Does the ocean know of the pull the moon has on its body, and of the tides it causes it to incessantly undergo?

Is it aware of the attractions and desires that draw and release it, over and over again?

Is the moon, that gazes down onto the ocean, aware that the light it shines so resplendently is in fact a reflection of the light of the sun, or does it think that that light is inherently its own?

As it watches over us from the skies, does the moon understand that without the sunshine it would not have the company of the starlight?

Does the sun that shines so bright onto the earth, bringing forth light and life, realise the intensity of the heat it casts upon the ocean causes its waters to painfully evaporate?

Is it aware of the suffering it causes the water to undergo, for it to become purified and cleansed?

Does the cloud that is then formed by this vapour, know of the place from whence it has come?

Does it remember the darkness deep beneath the ocean it once dwelt within before it could reign as prince of the sky, lofty and majestic?

When the burden of all it has witnessed during its reign becomes too much for it to bear and it breaks into tears, shedding itself across the land, do those droplets remember each other when they meet again in the rivers?

When those droplets merge to form a powerful torrent that washes away the timeless sorrows of the land, is it forging its own path through the land, or is the land humbly guiding the river back to its beloved?

As these rivers flow down to meet their beloved ocean, is the ocean aware of the selflessness with which the river sacrifices all he has, asking for nothing in return?

And as the waves of the ocean again carry this silent message from shore to shore, will we ever stop to contemplate and comprehend the truth that is latent within?

When will we come to understand the interconnected nature of our existence?

Will we ever become aware of the fact that we are the same entity existing in different forms?

Will the time come when we remember the previous forms that we once took for us to now be in our current state?

Will we ever come to recognise the infinite nature of our timeless existence?

At what point did we forget the singularity of our being? What leads us to believe that we can exist separately?

How can the ocean and the waves be separated, the sunshine and starlight differentiated?

Is the drop not the cloud? Is the ocean not the river? Are we not already that Oneness that we seek?

Are we not the sky to which we reach or the God of which you preach?

I rest my pen and cease my speech, for I have one final question and have never had anything to teach,

But tell me this,

Are you me or am I you, O Beloved One?

LIII

It is the fact that existence rests upon infinite dimensions simultaneously that causes you to perceive what you believe to be contradiction,

In actuality contradiction is merely a necessity of perception, the observer's restricted perspective creates the illusion of contradiction,

And this contradiction is in fact required in order to allow the perception in the first place,

For nothing could be perceived within this realm were it not for its seemingly contradictory nature,

The contradiction allows a thing to be witnessed in the first place, and unravelling it allows it to be understood for what it truly was,

At that point the false hypothesis of contradiction disappears, and the truth of the entity is revealed,

The paradox is, without the initial recognition of an entity in contradiction, the eventual unravelling and understanding would not, could not occur,

Were waves to not travel in their manner of ebb and flow, if sound did not vibrate equally above and below the axis of its travel, if light did not sway in the form of the wave as it travelled from sun to earth, then it could not be perceived, it could not be witnessed,

The state of contradiction is a necessary part of the observation of an object, idea, circumstance or emotion,

The perceived injustice of a particular circumstance brings it to light,

For if injustice had not been witnessed to exist, then what more would be justice than merely a state of nothingness?

And so it is, that in order for us to comprehend what it is that we truly are, we must first experience, that which we are not.

There is a log,
  There *is* a log,
 There is a log,
  And,
It has two choices,
  It *has* two choices,
 It has *two* choices,
It can decompose,
  It *can* decompose,
 It can decompose,
Itself and become one with the earth,
  Or,
It can burn,
  It *can* burn,
 It can burn,
And become light,
  But,
No matter which choice it makes,
  No matter *which* choice it makes,
 No matter which *choice* it makes,
It cannot escape the world of existence,

  For the earth gives life to the seed, and light gives life to the seedling,
  The earth gives life to the tree, and the light gives life to its leaves,
  The fruits of the tree are consumed by the hungry bird, just as the log was consumed by the thirsty fire,
  And that tree is then able to fly, its seeds being spread far and wide,
  Just as the light continues to travel even beyond our sight,

  Those seeds will one day meet the earth, again another tree is given birth,

So whether the log becomes light or earth, it will eventually become a tree again,

That tree will grow to give flowers and fruits, before long its leaves will again fall to the wind and its naked branches will fall to the earth,

Soon that tree will be gone, its presence will be no more, and in its place,

There is a log,

And as I stand there watching over this log, I realise I have two choices,

I always have two choices, but no matter which choice I make, I cannot escape this world of existence,

All I can do is transform,

From one form to the next, with each and every step and breath that I take, I have two choices,

Earth or light, water or air, learn or burn, now and then, here or there, love or fear,

And to this, there can be no end, for when travelling along a circle there can be no destination,

There can only be perpetual transformation.

LV

With continued reflection, meditation and remembrance you will activate each of the molecules of your form,

From there you can begin to, one by one, restore the powers you have always latently possessed,

You will remember how it was that the seed knew which way to sprout, how the dove knew which way to fly home and how the leaf knew how to dance and decompose,

You will be able to move and shape nature as your mind wishes, for your body is, and always has been, at one with the rest of the universe,

It is you who trick your mind into thinking otherwise,

Think of how your mind moves your arms, gives breath to your thoughts and reminds your heart to beat, because you know, feel and believe it all to be a part of your form,

So too, when you realise that you are forever intertwined with your universe, will you have influence over it,

Remind yourself of your interconnectedness, remove the imaginary boundaries of where you think your form begins and ends,

That you may once again move like the wind, fly like the bird and give fruits like the tree,

Once you recognise, comprehend, understand, know and believe, that you are one with your universe,

Then and only then, will you see what the moon sees as she watches you sleep,

Then and only then, will you feel the gentle caress shared between the clouds and the mountain's peak,

Then and only then, will you move the earth with the same effort that you move your limbs,

Then and only then, will you be ready for the day of our reunion.

LVI

The universe expanding is our gaining of understanding, the time and space this encapsulates is an experience that we ourselves create,

When the desire to know, prove and comprehend diminishes, dissolves and evaporates, so too then will the momentum of the expanding universe dissipate,

And we will begin our return towards a single point,

When the force which is *the intention to understand*, becomes equal and opposite to the force which is *the intention to become*, the universe would have completely lost its momentum,

We will come to a momentary standstill before beginning the journey back to The One,

When our quest for knowledge, the desire to investigate and comprehend the true essence of what we are,

Becomes equal to the strength of our collective belief in what it is that we always were,

Then and only then, will the paradoxes of this universe begin to truly unfurl,

At that point the universe would have arrived at the peak of its waveform, the point where velocity and acceleration are both zero, where action and intention are both nil,

For there will remain no more to be done, no more searching, inquiring or asking, only dreams to be fulfilled,

The momentary pause just before the inevitable return, the moment where we reflect upon all that humanity has learnt,

The point of stillness, that place of contentment, where our proof and faith, knowledge and belief, comprehension and trust are equal to each other,
Is where every secret is known and no untruth remains covered,

At that point the quest for knowing will be replaced with that of becoming, this is our collective midpoint, our halftime whistle,
Like a swimmer at the end of a lap pausing to turn and push off to return to the beginning,

When we reach this point we would have only achieved half of the purpose of our creation,
For becoming One, was what we actually wished for in that moment of separation,

At this point the mass of our knowledge, or rather the recognised parallels of our collectively acquired knowledge, will be so great, that we will finally reconise the oneness of their source,

This will begin to create a momentum that will propel us back to The Self, just as the planets gain momentum as they begin their journey back to the center of their reality,

Our momentum will increase, as our belief and trust in our inevitable destination pulls us back together, faster and faster as we gain faith in our glorious realisation,

The force of Love acting as gravity, will increase exponentially, as we approach our ultimate and inevitable glory,

The embodiment of our belief,

Now what would happen if such mass as is currently existing in our universe begins to accelerate towards itself without resisting?

Getting closer and closer, faster and faster, planets and solar systems unavoidable colliding and merging,

Trillions of once separated bodies joining and one single entity emerging,

Galaxies crashing as they all try to be the first to the central point of separation,

The universe collapsing in on itself, as it unravels the process of creation,

Oblivious that an inevitable impact with the rest of the universes looms,

Like a hoard of Boxing Day shoppers converging on a freshly revealed trolley of shoes,

Running faster and faster and faster until,
Booooom!!!!

They all reach the exact same point, at the exact same time, a moment of creation and destruction, both devastating and sublime,

I'm not exactly sure what might happen, as I can't yet remember experiencing such a thing,

But I'm guessing it would result in something like a big, bang?

I don't know, what do you think?

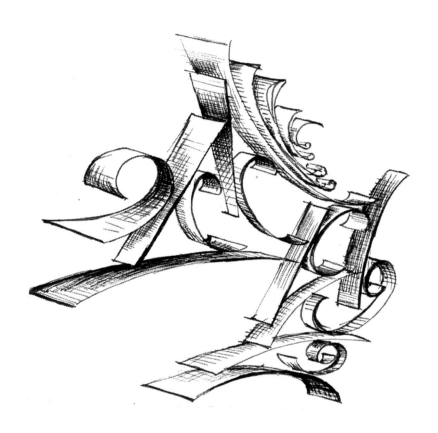

LVII

When I was young I heard my sister say, that with every breath we take, we get closer to the day we die,

So I held my breath and made her cry,

When I got older my mother told her that we die a little with every heart we break,

And that's how I became the walking dead,

Because I've broken so many hearts and had mine broken so many times,

I no longer know which pieces are yours and which pieces are mine,

I left a few pieces of me with her when I left that day, and I took a few pieces of her with me as I walked away,

Sometimes I feel so broken I fear there is nothing left of me to give, just pieces of a puzzle that don't seem to fit,

Like a broken vase that has offered its ashes to be taken by the wind,

I've sent pieces of myself far and wide and at times it seems I've spread myself too thin,

You see, this heart of mine was once a castle with a drawbridge and a moat,

Those inside were so loved that we barely even spoke,

With these hands of mine I would comfort, pray with and protect,

But these hands are now tired of fighting for Love, and the walls of that castle have been lost to neglect,

The rubble of the walls of that fortress have been shattered by the hammer of timelessness, so the castle of my heart became the finest of mists,

Covering the universe and everything within, that is why my heart can no longer hold anything in,

My Love can no longer hold firm to a single entity, like a Love drunk fool my heart can no longer see,
It lets in friend and enemy alike, because my heart can no longer differentiate wrong from right,

Its doors no longer exist for them to be closed, my heart is so broken it no longer knows,
To whom it belongs,

So I guess my Love is now truly blind and yet somehow it feels truly true,
For I don't care to know your past or your future, in fact I don't even care to know you,

Nor do I care to know your name, regardless of the fact I will Love you the same,

I don't care to know your gender, your religion or your race, because my Love, it has become like space,
Wherever you may go, my Love was already there,

Anything can rest beneath the dust of my Love, the more peaceful you are the sooner it will settle, the sooner it will flow,

But even if you are filled with hate, I will fill your lungs with Love as you take a deep breath to deal the deathblow,

I will smile as you withdraw your sword, I will praise your name as I fall,

For you need no invitation to enter my Love, my Love, wherever you may move you were already encompassed within it,

I do not care if your Love is discontinuous, overwhelming, fading or vivid,

For my Love knows nothing of reciprocation, and it is not the sun that decides to rise or set,

But the earth who turns her back to the sun as she continues to circumambulate,

So turn your back to me whenever you so choose, and turn to face to me whenever you may need,

My Love will remain as ever-present as the rays of the sun, but do not get too close my dear, unless you too wish to burn for me.

LVIII

Do you think that if this God you believe in were to actually exist, it would fit into the dark and narrow corridors of your minds?

And if perchance, God were to walk through your heart, have you thought to reflect on what this God of yours might find?

You clutter your hearts and minds with hatred and fear, with furnishings that do not belong,

Then you expect Love to come and rest with you, to sing to you of her song?

Nay, for the nightingale of Love sits upon the bow of the tree of life, but her song is a now broken sob,

For you have exiled her from her home and invited in her place every adornment except Love,

Instead of clearing yourself of judgment and condition, you continue to lay claim to possessions that are not yours,

You muddy your wings with the clay of earth so thick it leaves you incapable of winging your way back to the source,

You obsess over your physical appearance and wealth, seeking only to emphasise the differences between one another,

You follow the footsteps of your misguided forefathers and callously shed the blood of your brothers,

You fail to recognise we are one entity and that our physical forms are transitory,

You forget that God is what we once were, God is what we are, God cannot exist outside of us,

And still, eternal Love you continue to forsake for the sake of ephemeral lust.

LIX

I hope this will destroy you,

I hope these words with which I implore you, will break your
heart and scatter your mind,

Into pieces so small we will no longer know which pieces are
yours and which pieces are mine,

I want you to die to your ideas of self, so we can again fly
towards the One True Self,

I want you to burn like the wood becoming light, I want you to
learn there is no wrong or right,

Remind yourself it is not the sun that rises and sets, for he is
eternally still,

It is the earth who continues to turn her back to the sun of her
own free will,

As she orbits the object of her adoration,

Just as we turn our backs to the light, casting shadows before
us, searching for salvation,

But there is no God outside of Us, she is waiting patiently
inside, smiling as we cry,

For she knows that the suffering we endure is the true lover's
sacrifice,

Just as the moth who chose to selflessly burn, as it danced with
the flame,

It was out of Love that it gave its wings, and for this reason it
knew no pain,

It just wished for its soul like the smoke of its body, to rise to
the realm on high once again,

So burn for me my dear friends,

Burn for me until there is nothing left, just as the log waits
patiently by the fire for its turn to become light,

Wishing to be purged of its form so it too can wing its way
home, leave its body behind that its soul may merge with the souls of
others and together take flight,

So too, must we burn and transform through the seemingly haphazard happenings of life,

That we may return home and relieve our souls of this earthly strife,

And when we do, we leave our bodies to the custodianship of the earth,

For one day we may wish to return, that we may forget it all over again and once again learn,

Of the infinite nature of our being and the eternal essence of this dream within a dream,

So cry out no longer of whatever pains you may have come to endure,

Seek no more the company of the things of which you think you are sure,

For the river cannot take you to the ocean unless you release your hold of her banks,

And the graces of the hardships you have faced, you will not recognise until you are ready to give thanks,

So release your hold of your ideas of self, seek no more the comforts of earthly wealth,

Give yourself freely and without regard to the pull of the river, that you may start,

This journey on which your soul wishes to embark,

That at the end we may be together again,

Only to realise, this journey has had no beginning and it knows no end.

LX

Arise my Phoenix, arise, rise from the ashes of your life that you may return to the realm on high,

For you have burnt, sufficiently and obediently, you have for long enough, shed your impurities,

So arise my Phoenix, arise, the time has arrived for you to stretch your blessed wings and fly high,

Our separation has been prolonged, and I have longed for reunion for far too long,

So arise my Phoenix, arise, so you may rest your head in my hands and I can once again see the light of your eyes,

The moment has arrived, to take you by the hand and return you to the home to which you belong,

So arise my Phoenix, arise, let us once again be as One.

Lightning Source UK Ltd.
Milton Keynes UK
UKOW02f1245101014

239873UK00002B/43/P